WITNESS FOR A GENERATION

Witness for a
Generation

BY

JOHN J. BAER

Fithian Press · Santa Barbara · 1997

Published by Fithian Press
A division of Daniel and Daniel, Publishers, Inc.
Post Office Box 1525
Santa Barbara, CA 93102

Book design: Chris Putman

LIBRARY OF CONGRESS CATALOGING-IN-PUBLICATION DATA
Baer, John J., (date)
    Witness for a generation / by John J. Baer.
        p.   cm.
    ISBN 1-56474-219-9 (alk. paper)
    1. Baer, John J., (date). 2. Jews—California—Los Angeles—
Biography. 3. Refugees, Jewish—California—Los Angeles—Biography.
5. Jews—Poland—Wroclaw—Biography. 6. Jews, German—South
America—Biography. 7. Refugees, Jewish—South America—Biography.
I. Title.
F869.L89J5334 1997
979.4'94004924—dc21   97-10810
                                                            CIP
                                                            r97

*To the memory of my dear parents and their brothers and sisters,
who perished in the Holocaust.*

*To my unforgettable wife Ursula,
who inspired me to write my life's story.*

To my dear sister Lilli.

*To my dearest children, Gabriela and Leslie,
my grandchildren Michal, Tamar, Dan, and Julia,
my great-grandchild Ariella-Yael,
and to future generations of my family,
to remind them of their roots.*

*To my lovely wife Birgitta,
whose encouragement and support were
essential to the completion of this memoir.*

*To the people of the United States
in gratitude for giving my family and me a fresh start and a
new home in this beautiful country of freedom and opportunity,
and as a reminder that the price of liberty is perpetual vigilance.*

Contents

FOREWORD TO THE SECOND EDITION

WHEN THE FIRST EDITION of my book appeared in late 1997 I felt that I had discharged my obligation, as a survivor of the last generation of German Jewry, to give testimony of my personal experience of the cataclysmic events culminating in the Holocaust and of new beginnings in new lands. The response to my book was beyond my expectations and touched me deeply. There were letters and phone calls from readers, including some of my former classmates. There were searching and thought-provoking questions and comments from members of the audiences at my numerous book-signing presentations, which took me from Southern California all the way to the Holocaust Museum in Washington, D.C. A sampling of the sources of these communications, written and verbal, disclosed people of many ethnic origins and religious persuasions, including Germans and Austrians, particularly and encouragingly the second German and Austrian post-Holocaust generations, as well as former Jewish refugees from Germany and Austria and their children. While their perspective varied with their different backgrounds, they all received and understood my book in the spirit in which it was conceived: a message of hope and faith and a call to action. This response has encouraged me to proceed with the second edition of my book, in the hope that my message will reach an even wider readership.

C · h · a · p · t · e · r   O · n · e
CHILDHOOD AND YOUTH

I WAS BORN ON APRIL 26, 1917, in Breslau, the capital of Silesia, Germany. My father, Bernhard Baer, was born in the former German province of Posen, son of Yizchak Baer and Blume Baer. My great-grandfather's original name had been Beer Isaac. His family changed their name at the time of the emancipation of the Prussian Jews in 1812.

My mother's name was Marta, daughter of Jacob and his wife, Babette Block. She was born near the city of Ratibor, Upper Silesia.

The year 1917 was the fourth year of World War I, during which imperial Germany was locked in deadly battle with the western powers and with tsarist Russia. Four members of my immediate family had joined the Kaiser's armies to defend the "Fatherland," which less than thirty years later, under Nazi rule, would pay us back in its own way.

Two of my uncles on my mother's side, who had volunteered for military service, were killed in action in Poland and East Prussia.

One of my father's brothers, my Uncle Gerson, was taken prisoner in France. My fourth uncle, Alfred Block, my mother's brother, who fought until 1918, was decorated for bravery.

In 1920 or 1921, as a result of the Treaty of Versailles, a

plebiscite took place to determine whether Upper Silesia, where my mother and her sisters were born, should be ceded to Poland or remain German. Everyone born in Upper Silesia was entitled to vote. I still remember my mother telling me that she and her sisters, who were active in an association called Verein Heimattreuer Oberschlesier (Association of Loyal Upper Silesians), would travel to Upper Silesia in order to cast their votes in favor of Germany. Although the plebiscite ended in favor of Germany, a large slice of Upper Silesia was awarded to Poland.

My childhood and adolescence were marked by the turbulent years of the Weimar Republic, which succeeded the Kaiser in 1918.

I grew up together with my sister Lilli, born in 1915, who, albeit unfairly perhaps, was blamed for many of the pranks which I played as a boy, simply because she was the "elder sister who should have watched over your younger brother." I believe that she has meanwhile forgiven me.

One of these many pranks, which I remember even to this day, occurred in a public park where my sister and I were playing. When I got bored of playing in the sand box I started walking around and noticed a red box attached to a pole. The red box had a glass front, behind which one could see a handle. Believing that this was a candy vending machine, I broke the glass and pulled the handle. After a while we heard the sirens of approaching firetrucks. A few minutes later these trucks rolled up to the edge of the park. Out jumped the firemen looking for a fire to extinguish. Pretty soon they found the culprit. My dad had to pay a fine, and I was taken to the woodshed.

After leaving school, Lilli entered my mother's millinery store, where she learned the millinery trade. She got married on August 24, 1938, in a double ceremony joined by my parents, who celebrated their silver wedding anniversary. This was the last joyful gathering of my family and our relatives. I emigrated four months later. My sister and her husband left for Melbourne, Australia, in March 1939. There they had one child, Michael, who showed great musical promise at an early age. He started his musical career as cantor at one of the major synagogues in Melbourne. Subsequently, he became an opera singer in Kaiserslautern, Germany, and settled in Frankfurt. His repertory ranges from Richard Wagner's *Meistersinger*, and *Tristan und Isolde*, to *Fiddler on the Roof*. His engagements take him not only across Europe, but also back to his native Australia, where he got high marks from the critics for his performance at the Sydney Opera House.

I began grammar school (*Vorschule*) in 1923. Although as a six-year-old boy I was not, at the time, aware of the political turmoil which had gripped Germany in the years following the military collapse, I recall very vividly the galloping inflation which raged in Germany beginning in 1922. One day when I wanted to buy a simple pen from the little stationery store near my grammar school, I was told that the price had just gone up to one million Deutschmark. I remember the day when my father opened up a leather pouch, tossed out all of its contents of banknotes, and told me that I was free to paper the walls with them. He told me later that the pouch contained all of our family's savings.

After only three years at grammar school, I was permitted to skip the fourth year due to my superior grades. I was admitted to the Johannes-Gymnasium, a humanistic Gymnasium which emphasized the classical languages, Latin and Greek. I started with Latin, which never gave me any trouble, and studied it for nine years. Two years later, I could elect between English and French. I opted for French, with which I have maintained a love affair ever since. One year later I tackled ancient Greek, which, despite its rather complicated grammar, I enjoyed studying for the next six years. It opened up the world of Homer, Aeschylus, Sophocles, Euripides, and Aristophanes, depicting man's battle against fate. Later on I was introduced to Plato and his philosophy, his *Republic* and other writings. I was deeply impressed by his *Apologia*, which describes Socrates' "defense" against the indictment by an Athenian jury charging him with corrupting Athenian youth and spreading disrespect for the gods. All this was a mere cover-up for the attempt by Athens' rulers to silence a man who stood up against injustice and corruption of the democratic system, irrespective of personal consequences. In the course of history, others would from time to time light the same torch for truth and justice in defiance of the sound and fury of the populace and its prejudices.

During the sixth year of my studies at the Gymnasium, I took up the English language. I had an excellent instructor in French and in English, who laid very particular emphasis on proper pronunciation and intonation. To this end, he used illustrations and pictures that he himself had drawn. I remember one that portrayed an Englishman in a golf outfit holding a pipe in his mouth and slowly descending the stairs. "This," he said, "is the way English sounds to the beginner." Another picture showed a little man with a black goatee racing up and down the stairs. "This," he said, "is the way French sounds to the uninitiated." The last picture was concealed by a paper flap. When he lifted the flap, you could see a dog who appeared to be barking. "This," he said, pointing to the dog, "is the way German sounds to the rest of the world." A highly debatable description of the language of Goethe and Schiller.

However, little did I or anybody else realize that this was indeed the way a former corporal in the German army with a little moustache and a raised arm would sound to the rest of the world when he addressed the frenzied masses in Germany a few years later.

In addition to languages, I liked the study of English, French, and German literature. I likewise took an abiding interest in history, although the history textbooks and most of the professors' comments reflected the view that World War I had been forced upon Germany and that England and France had plotted to "get even" with "us Germans."

The German poet who impressed me most was Friedrich Schiller, the advocate of individual and collective freedom. I learned to appreciate Goethe much later, and to this day I have found his *Faust* to be an inexhaustible source of introspection into man's struggle for self-redemption.

Math—that is, arithmetic, algebra, geometry—and physics were not exactly my cup of tea. One of our math professors was the target of numerous pranks in which I was a prominent participant. He once told us that he was one of the few people who understood Einstein's theory of relativity. In fact he frequently referred to himself and Albert Einstein as "I and my friend Einstein."

One day during a math lesson there was a knock on the classroom door. I volunteered to open the door and came back with the announcement "Herr Professor, Einstein is outside." Incredulous, Professor Juettner opened the door. What he saw was a good solid rock. By way of explanation to those who are not familiar with German, I wish to add that the name "Einstein" means "a rock." When the professor demanded that the pranksters get up from their seats, the whole class arose. We were all sentenced to two hours extra time after classes.

Every afternoon except Thursdays we had to prepare the assignments given us by our professors, which usually took at least three or four hours. There were no assignments to be prepared for Friday. Instead, on Thursday afternoon we could elect either to play volleyball at the stadium or to work in the school garden (irreverently called by us the "Onion Club"—*Zwiebelklub*). There each student had a special plot where he was expected to raise tomatoes, radishes, and other vegetables. I opted for the school garden. After a few months I grew tired of the long streetcar ride from our home to the school garden. I made arrangements with one of my schoolmates, who lived about ten minutes from the school garden, to take care of my plot for compensation. A few months later, during an unforeseen inspection of the garden by the principal, the scheme was discovered and I was read the riot act.

I was never a good sportsman, except for skiing. I still remember the skiing excursions to the Silesian mountains called Riesengebirge, a mountain range which forms part of the Sudeten chain, forming the border between Germany and Czechoslovakia. There were extra weekend trains for skiers, which left at about 7:00 A.M. and arrived in the mountains about three hours later. We climbed on the trains while it was still pitch dark and everybody was sleepy. Pretty soon, at dawn, everybody came back to life. The sweet smell of fresh rolls mixed with the aroma of fresh coffee from the thermos bottles, and the sound of *Wanderlieder* accompanied by harmonica players created a joyful mood with readiness for a day on the slopes.

Later in the day, when darkness fell, everybody got together in one of the *Bauden* (inns) for the five o'clock tea and dancing in ski attire.

I had several friends among my classmates. My best friend was named Fritz Pasch. He was the son of an ear-nose-and-throat specialist. We shared many experiences, among which were those which adolescents face once they discover the attractions of the opposite sex and literature on sexual subjects, which their parents erroneously believe to have been safely hidden from their view. One such book was authored by Vandervelde, a forerunner of the American Kinsey, who wrote the *Kinsey Reports* in the 1940s. Fritz and I belonged to the *Kameraden*, a boy scout group of predominantly Jewish composition. We enjoyed excursions through the woods that lined the banks of the Oder River, where we lit campfires and enjoyed good potato soups and sausages, followed by the singing of various boy scout songs to the strains of the guitar. A large portion of this repertory consisted of patriotic songs and songs attributed to the armies of mercenaries (*Landsknechte*) of the sixteenth and seventeenth centuries.

My friend Fritz left Germany in 1934 and went to trade school in Holland, where he was subsequently hired by Phillips in Eindhoven. When the Germans overran Holland, he and his girlfriend fled on bikes across Belgium to France, where Fritz was interned in the infamous Gurs (St. Cyprien) camp after France's surrender to the Germans. I learned after the war that Fritz had escaped from Gurs camp and found refuge with a French farmer. Apparently he was betrayed a few months later, and the French police appeared at the farmer's home, arrested Fritz, and delivered him to the

Gestapo, who deported him to Auschwitz.

Fritz's parents survived the war in Holland, where they were hidden by a Dutch family.

Another friend of mine was Helmut Gins, who was an excellent student. He studied for the rabbinate at the Jewish Theological Seminary in Breslau, and was ordained as rabbi.

During the Kristallnacht pogroms, Helmut was arrested and taken to the Buchenwald concentration camp. He never overcame the traumatic effect of his experiences in that camp. He subsequently emigrated to La Paz, Bolivia, where I saw him again upon my arrival from Peru. We shared a small room until my future wife, Ursula, arrived from England. He had become a different person, a loner who was unable to cope with his responsibilities as rabbi and spiritual leader of a congregation consisting entirely of Jewish immigrants. He avoided social contact, even with Ursula and me. After our departure from Bolivia, he obtained a pulpit with a small Jewish congregation in northern Brazil. Shortly after his arrival there, he ended his life.

My third friend, Guenther (Bibi) Mott, whom I met when he had to repeat the third grade at the Gymnasium, came from a mixed marriage. His father, a dentist, had composed the music for a popular operetta entitled *Viktoria und ihr Husar* (*Victoria and her Hussar*). Bibi had an elder sister, a beautiful girl on whom I soon developed a crush. Bibi was very musical and always sang the latest hit songs. He didn't take school and teachers very seriously and was of great help to me in performing numerous pranks upon our teachers. Thanks to his mother's connections with the management of the principal stage theaters in Breslau, she often obtained complimentary theater tickets, of which Bibi and I were the beneficiaries. The Breslau theaters were well known for their excellent actors. I still vividly remember the impressive performances of *Richard III*, Schiller's *Wallenstein*, *William Tell*, *The Captain of Koepenick* (*Der Hauptmann von Koepenick*), and George Bernard Shaw's *Saint Joan*, a satire on Joan of Arc.

Bibi quit school at an early age and went to work for a store that sold musical publications. Thanks to arrangements made by Bibi's sister, who had moved to St. Gallen, Switzerland, Bibi spent the war years in Switzerland, the only survivor among my close friends. We always remained in contact, and in 1961, when I visited Germany for the first time, we had a reunion. Bibi is now retired in Ronco, near Ascona, Switzerland, where I visited him and his wife, Martha, in their beautiful villa, Sponda Bella, overlooking Lago Maggiore. Nearby is the little Ronco cemetery, the last resting place of Bibi's mother and also of the German writer Erich-Maria Remarque, author of *All Quiet on the Western Front* (*Im Westen Nichts Neues*). Bibi's mother was a woman of true character and courage. During the dark days following Kristallnacht in November 1938, she came to see my mother to express her condolences. I well remember her words on that occasion: "I am ashamed of being a German." She kept inviting her Jewish friends to her musical soirees, in defiance of the threats she received from the Nazis.

The curriculum in the German public school system included religious instruction in various faiths. During the first three years of my studies at the Gymnasium, our instructor in Jewish religion was an Orthodox rabbi who was knowledgeable not only in Jewish subjects but in the humanities as well. However, he was extremely intolerant toward those of us whose views did not embrace Orthodoxy.

The Johannes Gymnasium had a long tradition of liberal-minded professors, several of whom were Jewish and outstanding in their respective fields. Approximately 25 percent of the students were also Jewish.

Every week I also attended religious school at the "New Synagogue," a house of worship of the Reform sect of the Jewish community of Breslau. There I studied Hebrew and was introduced to the prayers and liturgy.

My parents were of the Liberal Jewish persuasion. Every Friday evening my mother lit the Sabbath candles and said the prayer over our beautiful silver candleholders, followed by my dad's recital of the blessing of wine and bread, and a festive Sabbath meal.

One of the religious highlights of the year was the Passover seder, conducted by my dad in Hebrew. We observed the high holidays—Rosh Hashana and Yom Kippur—during which my parents' places of business were closed. My parents, my sister, and I walked to the synagogue together, all dressed for the holidays. My father, like most other worshippers, wore a top hat and a dark suit. Everybody was in a festive mood and emotionally receptive to the solemn services, which found their most beautiful expression in Lewandowsky's melodies chanted on the high holidays.

My parents shared the belief held by the overwhelming majority of German Jews that they were Germans like their Christian fellow-citizens and that Judaism was exclusively a matter of religion. They honestly believed that the emancipation of German Jews was an accomplished and irrevocable fact, and that whatever anti-Semitism remained in Germany would disappear with the progress of democratic institutions. They believed that the Fatherland would be mindful of the contributions and sacrifices made by the German Jews who fought for their country in World War I. To most German Jews, Zionism, which considered the emancipation of Jews in the Western countries an illusion and which sought to establish a national home for the Jews in Palestine, appeared to be a throwback to the ghetto era.

The number of outstanding German-Jewish men and women who made lasting contributions to their country in all spheres of public life, as well as in the arts and sciences, far outweighed their numerical proportion of less than 1 percent of Germany's total population. To name but a few: Albert Einstein, whose impact on science needs no description; Paul Ehrlich, who invented Salvasan, the first effective remedy for syphilis; Professor Fritz Haber, whose invention of a nitrogen formula usable as a fertilizer enabled Germany to survive the allied blockade that cut it off from the supply of Chilean saltpeter during World War I; Emil Rathenau, the founder of AEG (the German version of General Electric); his son Walter Rathenau, the first foreign minister of the Weimar Republic, who negotiated the peace treaty between Germany and the

Soviet Union in 1922. He was assassinated by anti-Semitic thugs a short time afterwards; Albert Ballin, founder of the HAPAG (Hamburg-America Steamship Company), a close friend of Kaiser Wilhelm II; Ferdinand Lassalle, born in Breslau, founder of the German Social Democratic Party; Hugo Preuss, chief architect of the constitution of the Weimar Republic; and many others too numerous to mention.

The city of Breslau had a population of approximately 600,000, about the size of San Francisco. It was one of the oldest cities in the southeastern part of Germany and traced its origin to the tenth century. It had changed masters a few times, from Poland to Bohemia, Austria, and then to Prussia in 1740. In 1945, it was ceded to Poland. The city, called Wroclaw today, owes its importance to its location at the crossroads of the trade routes between the Baltic and the Adriatic from north to south and between Germany, Poland, and Russia from west to east.

Jewish merchants had been prominent in building up this trade, and the first Jewish settlers had inhabited Breslau and the rest of Silesia in the twelfth century. In 1453, the citizenry was whipped up against the Jews by the itinerant fanatical Dominican monk, San Juan Capistrano. All Jews who were not able to flee and who were unwilling to convert, were burned at the stake. A few decades later, some Jewish merchants returned. However, their numbers were severely restricted by the authorities.

During the second half of the eighteenth century, under Prussian rule, the Jewish community of Breslau began to grow. When emancipation of the Prussian Jews was proclaimed in 1812, there was a sizeable Jewish community there. Breslau was well known throughout central Europe as an outstanding center of Jewish learning and scholarship.

In Breslau, the split between the Orthodoxy, led by Tiktin and Samson Raphael Hirsch, two eminent Orthodox Jewish scholars, and the emerging Jewish Liberal movement, under the leadership of Abraham Geiger, first broke into the open and threatened to tear the Jewish community asunder.

Subsequently, however, the integration of the Breslau Jewish community, consisting of the Orthodox, Conservative, and Liberal persuasions, was restored and consolidated as an *Einheitsgemeinde* (United congregation). This enabled Jews of different religious orientations to come together in one organization.

Interestingly enough, while there was freedom of worship in Weimar Germany, it was the state that collected the so-called church or synagogue taxes. Jews who did not wish to be assessed these taxes had to officially sever their ties with Judaism. While this system did not meet our American constitutional standards of separation of church and state, it ensured the independence of the rabbis from the vagaries of "temple politics" that plague many Jewish congregations in the United States and that degrade those who should be spiritual leaders to fundraisers and politicians serving at the whim of a board of trustees dominated by a few financially influential members.

During the 1920s and 1930s, when I grew up, the Jewish population of Breslau numbered close to 30,000. The most prominent house of worship was the New Synagogue, a beautiful structure with a cupola. It was erected around 1870, and had become one of Breslau's landmarks. In addition, there was the so-called Storch Synagogue, maintained by the Conservatives. The Orthodox had numerous small synagogues called *Betstuben.* Each synagogue had its own religious school. I attended the school maintained by the New Synagogue.

We lived on the fourth floor of an apartment house at 109 Viktoriastrasse, in an upper-middle-class residential area. Looking onto the street from our living room one saw a cigar store, a gourmet shop with the finest chocolates in the neighborhood, and a bakery where my dad used to buy rolls for breakfast. Next to the bakery was Herr Josef Mueller's barber shop, where gentlemen, while getting their shaves or haircuts, settled the world's affairs and were treated to the latest neighborhood gossip. At the end of the block was a taxistand, which, until the mid-1920s, had served horse-drawn coaches with the coachmen in their lacquered top hats sitting in the boxes.

Around the corner of our block was the district police station. Like all other police stations throughout Germany, it kept a register of all persons residing in its district. Everybody who moved into the district had to register there, and whenever somebody moved out of the district, he, she, or the family had to notify the police in person. This meticulous record-keeping of all the residents by the police made it easy for the Gestapo and the SS to maintain strict surveillance over all residents after Hitler's takeover, and to quickly locate and apprehend Jews or any other political suspects at any time.

My father was a sales representative for a fur company headquartered in Berlin. He also represented several textile manufacturers. My mother, together with her younger sister, Alma, owned and operated one of the top-ranking *Putzsalons* (millinery stores) in town. My mother was the business head of the enterprise, while my aunt, who had done her apprenticeship and professional training in Luxembourg and Paris, was in charge of selecting the latest designs of ladies' hats.

My parents worked extremely hard to make a living for our family. One of their main concerns was our education. The first subject at the dinner table was always our day in school. Since I was not the world's greatest mathematician, my father, who was rather good at math, was of great help to me. He showed a great deal of patience in explaining to me the computation of percentages. He was also knowledgeable in history, particularly modern history. My mother was steeped in poetry and folklore. My parents frequently went to see our teachers in order to find out about our progress (or lack of it).

On Sunday afternoons in summer, our parents would take my sister and me to the beautiful parks in the southern part of Breslau, where we would spend the afternoon in conversation with our relatives over coffee and cake. In winter we went to a *Konditorei* (cafe), where one could sit for hours with one's friends and relatives discussing the affairs of the world over coffee and delicious pastries.

My parents maintained close ties with our relatives who lived in Breslau, including my mother's four sisters, their husbands and children.

My mother's brother, Alfred, and his family lived in Magdeburg, a six-hour train ride from Breslau. He had a lovely wife named Erna and three children—two girls, Gerda and Lotte, and a son, Peter. Our families visited each other frequently. During my first train trip to Magdeburg with my mother, in 1923, a man entered our compartment and announced that the French had just occupied the Rhineland. I got up and exclaimed "Sir, what do the French look like? Let's get them." My mother never tired of telling this anecdote.

My uncle's daughter Gerda, of whom I was particularly fond, emigrated to South Africa in 1935 to get married to her former boyfriend, who had left Germany a couple of years before. My cousin Lotte met a tragic end. She went to London in early 1938. Suddenly, on or about November 7, 1938, my uncle received a telegram informing him that she had suddenly died. He obtained a visa from the British Consulate General and left for London on November 8, 1938. The following day, in the course of the Kristallnacht, the Gestapo went to his apartment to arrest him. Under the circumstances, he was permitted to stay in England, where he lived until after the war. His daughter's tragic end probably saved his life.

My cousin Peter, who must have been about fifteen years old at the time, went to live with his aunt in Hamburg, where he saw me off to the boat on my way to South America. He became an engineer and after the war went to Toronto, Canada, where he now lives in retirement with his wife Helen.

On my father's side, there were three brothers and one sister. One of his brothers, named Gerson, had married a distant cousin of my mother's and lived in Upper Silesia, where he operated a general store. His two remaining brothers and a sister named Johanna lived in a village near my father's birthplace, Lindenheim, which had been part of the former Prussian province of Posen, ceded to Poland in 1919 pursuant to the Treaty of Versailles. They owned and operated the only general store in a brick building that also served them as living quarters. The building was surrounded by a beautiful orchard of cherry, apple, and plum trees as well as by berry patches. They also operated a farm and a stable with a horse, a cow, and plenty of chickens. They had their own butter churner, with which I experimented from time to time; however, I never had enough patience to wait until the butter solidified, and the finished product was not exactly fit for human consumption.

For many years our family—that is, my parents, my sister, and I—spent our summer vacations with our aunt and uncles in Lindenheim, renamed Smieszkowo after the Polish takeover. These summer vacations are among my earliest and fondest memories. Our relatives were loving people and spoiled us kids rotten. My Aunt Johanna, who was unmarried, managed the business, which was licensed to dispense alcoholic beverages. She was a hardy soul and certainly knew how to deal with all sorts of people, including Polish officialdom and those who insisted upon "one last glass of schnapps."

I thoroughly enjoyed the horse-and-buggy rides with my Uncle Julius whenever he went to the nearby town of Czarnkow, which was on the German-Polish border marked by the Netze River. Many of these trips included the delivery of grain harvested from our fields to the flour mills. Often Uncle Julius let me hold the reins, even though the horse had his own way with me!

Like many middle-sized towns in the Prussian province of Posen, Czarnkow had a substantial Jewish population. Jewish learning and observance of the Sabbath and the other Jewish holidays were long-standing traditions. It is no coincidence that the province of Posen gave German Jewry some of its most prominent leaders, such as the venerated Rabbi Leo Baeck, who later on went to Berlin, where he became the spiritual leader of German Jewry in its darkest hour. It was Rabbi Baeck who refused to leave his persecuted fellow Jews as they were about to be taken to the concentration camps. He went with them to Theresienstadt in Czechoslovakia and miraculously survived the war.

Near the center of Czarnkow stood the synagogue, a large brick building. Every Saturday morning during my yearly visits to my relatives, I got up early and walked down the country road from Szmieszkowo (Lindenheim) to Czarnkow, a distance of about four miles, past cornfields, meadows, and forests. Shortly before reaching Czarnkow, I passed the old Jewish cemetery on my right, where my great-grandparents and my grandparents were buried. I always reached the synagogue in time for the reading from the Torah, to which I was called to say the *berachot* (blessings). It was in this synagogue that my ancestors had worshipped and where my father became bar mitzvah in 1891, shortly before he left his parents' home to become an apprentice in the leading department stores in Leipzig and Berlin. My father's school principal had tried to prevail upon my grandfather to let my father finish high school and attend institutions of higher learning, since my father happened to be an excellent student of great promise. Unfortunately, however, since my grandparents had numerous children to support from a rather meager income, they could not comply with the principal's request.

After the end of the Sabbath morning services, I was usually invited by my father's cousins who lived in Czarnkow to share the Sabbath meal with them. After lunch everyone enjoyed an afternoon snooze, and the streets became deserted in the hot midday sun. A few hours later things came back to life, with relatives and friends visiting each other, while I started the long trek back home on the dusty country road.

Although on the surface life seemed to be rather quiet and uneventful in the territories of western Poland, that country was infested by virulent anti-Semitism long before Hitler seized power in Germany. The Jewish population in Poland, which amounted to approximately three million before 1939, was constantly subjected to repressive laws and practices in economy and politics. Under the quota system of the *numerus clausus* practiced by the universities, only a small number of Jews were permitted to attend college or university in Poland. They were physically segregated from the other students in special sections and subjected to all sorts of harassment. The Catholic Church, which was very influential in Poland, was the main source of anti-Semitism. I vividly remember one day when, during my visit to Czarnkow, I saw a Catholic priest address a large crowd in the main square. This cleric, one of the princes of the Polish Church, admonished the faithful not to have anything to do with the Jews who had killed "our Saviour."

Many years later I read a book by Jerzy Kozinsky entitled *The Painted Bird.* In this book the author describes a scene in which a Polish peasant watching the black smoke rise from the crematoria at Auschwitz remarks, "The Jews are finally paying the penalty for crucifying our Lord, Jesus Christ." When I read these lines I remembered the Catholic cleric addressing the crowd in the marketplace in Czarnkow.

Meanwhile, I continued my studies at the Johannes Gymnasium. Even under the Weimar regime there always was a noticeable degree of anti-Semitism in Germany, sparked mainly by the extreme right-wing parties, specifically by the National Socialist Party, which created and spread the myth that Germany had not been defeated by the Allies on the battlefield, but had been stabbed in the back by Jews and communists.

Who would have thought that the lunatic with the little moustache who screamed his head off when he spoke in public would one day become a hero to a majority of Germans? He was not even a German, having been born in Braunau, Austria. Accordingly, he had to be naturalized in order to become a full-fledged German. Who would waste his time reading his trashy book entitled *Mein Kampf?*

C · h · a · p · t · e · r   T · w · o

COLLAPSE

WE WERE ON OUR SUMMER vacation with my parents in 1930 when my dad told us that one of the largest German banks, if not the largest, had collapsed and closed its doors. This set off a "run" on German banks by depositors who wanted to withdraw their accounts. The banks were unable to cope with this situation and closed their counters. Quite a few of them collapsed, and the German economy, which only a few weeks previously appeared to be on the road to recovery from the postwar nightmare, lapsed into its deepest depression. Factories and offices closed *en masse*, and millions of unemployed roamed the streets or stood in line in front of the government offices for their dole.

I recall that my Uncle Gerson, who operated a general store in Upper Silesia, which was dependent mainly on the coal miners' business, visited us and asked my father for financial help, since he had to close his store as a result of the shutdown of the mines.

Economic chaos brought political disaster. In the October 1930 Reichstag elections, the Nazis gained a large number of seats.

German cities were inundated by Nazi propaganda, and storm troopers appeared in the streets battling with communists as both parties promised the unemployed *Arbeit und Brot* (work and bread). Anti-Semitic propaganda, which held the Jews accountable for the economic disaster, increased sharply. "Emergency Decrees" (*Notverordnungen*) issued by the Bruening administration in Berlin followed each other in short order, but nothing helped as things got worse and worse.

On January 30, 1933, while my class was on a lunch break at a restaurant during a skiing excursion, an announcement came over the radio that Reichspraesident von Hindenburg, the president of the German Republic and an arch-conservative hero of World War I, had called upon Hitler to form a new cabinet as Chancellor of the Reich. Some of the Nazis in the audience cheered, but many others had mixed feelings. Some said that perhaps it was a good idea to challenge Hitler to either put up or shut up in finding a solution to the intractable problem of massive unemployment.

That night, Nazi stormtroopers marched through all German cities in torchlight parades celebrating what they called the "National Awakening." The Nazi government lost no time in tightening its grip on Germany. Its first measures were the exclusion of the Jews from all government positions and from most of the professions.

A few weeks later the Nazis organized a nationwide book-burning event. The stormtroopers lit a bonfire in one of the main squares of Breslau. In the presence of a huge and enthusiastic crowd, they proceeded to toss books written by "Jewish Bolshevist" authors such as Heinrich Heine, Thomas Mann, and Sigmund Freud into the flames.

On April 1, 1933, the day that has become known as "Boycott Day," Nazi storm troopers stood in front of all Jewish business establishments throughout Germany with placards asking people not to buy from Jews. I still vividly recall the two uniformed Nazis standing in front of my mother's store with posters bearing the inscription *Kauft nicht bei Juden* (Don't buy from Jews).

My world, our world, the world of German Jewry founded upon the belief that we had acquired an inalienable right to German citizenship, collapsed overnight. Some of our friends committed suicide. Many of the leaders of German Jewry admonished us not to despair and intimated that the cataclysm that engulfed us might well be temporary. However, harsh reality and the gradual disenfranchisement of German Jews by the Nazi government gave the lie to this self-deception.

In the midst of this atmosphere of doom, I remember one uplifting voice. It was that of the *Juedische Rundschau* (*Jewish Review*), the official paper of the Zionist movement in Germany. In April 1933, under the headline "*Tragt ihn mit Stolz, den gelben Fleck*" ("Wear it with pride—the Yellow Badge"), it challenged the German Jews to hold their heads high, to take pride in their heritage, and to devote all of their strength to supporting the establishment of a Jewish national home in Palestine.

I searched for a new meaning and a new definition of myself as a Jew, as well as for an explanation of the catastrophe that had engulfed us. Heated discussions took place within our family, among my friends, and among the members of the German-Jewish Youth Movement, the Jewish youth organization to which I belonged. My parents and relatives and, in fact, the majority of the older generation refused to accept that this was the beginning of the end of the so-called German Jewish symbiosis.

In school there were few changes at first, except that the principal of my Gymnasium, an anti-Nazi, was removed immediately. At the time of Hitler's assumption of power, in January 1933, I was still two years away from my final examination, similar in nature to the French *baccalaureat*. Gradually, I and the other Jewish students began to feel isolated, as most of our "Aryan" schoolmates avoided any social contact with us. Many of our professors appeared with the swastika armband and gave the Nazi salute at the beginning of every school session.

One of the most humiliating experiences, which I still remember very vividly today, was the mandatory visit by all students, including Jewish students, to an exhibit on the subject of *Rassenkunde* (race science). This exhibit was dedicated to the Nazi doctrine of the superiority of the Aryan race and the inferiority of other groups, particularly Jews. They attempted to "prove" this theory by displaying pictures and photos of outstanding Germans, including Goethe and Beethoven (whose features were anything but typically German), and contrasting them with caricatures of "typical Jews."

I had not yet decided what I would do after leaving the Gymnasium. I was very much interested in languages. I was already fluent in French and had a good knowledge of English, and in addition had studied Polish at the Slavic Languages Institute at Breslau. I was interested in foreign affairs and, prior to Hitler, had considered becoming a foreign correspondent for one of the liberal German newspapers. On the other hand, since I also had a deep interest in Jewish history and religion, I had likewise considered studying for the rabbinate. It seemed that Hitler helped me make up my mind. I decided to study for the rabbinate after passing the *Abitur* in March 1935, the youngest student of my class to do so. Next to the California bar examination, this was the toughest exam I ever took in my life.

The Abitur exam consisted of written and oral parts; the latter included one elective subject and another subject that was not disclosed before the exam. My elective oral exam was French naturalism, specifically Guy de Maupassant and Zola, on whom I gave a dissertation in French. I was also examined in history, specifically the Bismarck era, with equally good results.

Breslau had one of the oldest, if not the oldest, Jewish theological seminaries in Germany. Founded in 1846, the seminary was renowned the world over for outstanding scholars who had given it prominence. Suffice it to say that Heinrich Graetz, the author of *History of the Jews*, Manual Joel, and, last but not least, Ephraim Urbach, later president of the Hebrew University in Jerusalem, were among those responsible for the excellence in scholarship and the profound influence this institution had on Jewish life throughout Germany.

Throughout our history, we Jews have risen to the challenge of persecution by helping each other and by strengthening the knowledge of and pride in our spiritual and cultural heritage.

In his story entitled "The Rabbi of Bacharach," Heinrich Heine described the life of the Jewish community in the little town of Bacharach on the Rhine as follows: "The more they were beset with hatred from without, the more fond and tender grew the Bacharach Jews' domestic life, and the more profound their piety and fear of God."

This was accomplished during the Nazi era by the expansion of Jewish schools and study groups on Judaism and other subjects. In addition, an institution by the name of Kulturbund came into being, featuring plays, concerts, and lectures presented by top-notch Jewish artists and scholars.

The Kulturbund events in Breslau took place at the Freundesaal, a hall previously used only for social events. After the November 1938 pogroms, the Nazis prohibited all Jewish cultural events. In 1941, at the time of the deportations of the remaining Jews to the death camps in Poland, the Freundesaal was used as a gathering place for deportees before their shipment to the railroad station and on to the camps.

After completing the Abitur, I became extremely active in Jewish political life. The belief held by a vast majority of German Jews that they were Germans first and that Judaism was merely a matter of religious belief (or, in many cases, a nonbelief) received a shattering blow when Hitler came to power. Suddenly the prophetic words of Theodor Herzl, creator of the Zionist movement, "We are *one* people" and "The majority of the population determines who is a stranger in the land" (*"Wer der Fremde im Lande ist, das entscheidet die Mehrheit"*) began to acquire meaning for those of us who had advocated assimilation as the solution to the "Jewish problem." As a young student I enrolled in the Jewish fraternity named Ivriah and soon thereafter joined the Betar, the youth group of the Zionist-Revisionist Movement. What attracted me to this movement was its uncompromising adherence to the basic tenet of Zionism, which was the creation of a Jewish state supported by a Jewish majority in Eretz Israel.

I was deeply impressed by the speeches and publications authored by Zev Jabotinsky, the leader of the Zionist-Revisionists and the creator of the Jewish Legion in World War I. Jabotinsky predicted that the Jewish state would not come as a result of fraternization with the Arabs, but would have to be fought for and would require military preparedness of the Jewish population in what was then Palestine. In short order, I became the leader of the Betar Youth Movement in Breslau.

At the same time, I pursued my studies at the Jewish Theological Seminary in Breslau for about three years with great interest and good results. Nevertheless, under the influence of my studies of philosophy, specifically that of Baruch Spinoza, I began to develop my own ideas about God and the universe, which were not in accord with the traditional Jewish concept of a personal God who had revealed Himself at Mount Sinai. After thorough reflection, I concluded that I would not fit into the role of a rabbi. I decided to apply for admission to Breslau University, a most difficult undertaking, since the Nazi regime had reduced the "quota" of Jewish students at Breslau University to a total of two. But as a result of my scholastic record and the recommendation of one of my former professors at the Gymnasium, I was admitted to the university and attended courses in Romance languages and literature (French, Spanish, and Italian), philosophy, and economics, for about two and a half years, until Kristallnacht on November 9, 1938.

I believe it was in the summer of 1937 that I met my companion for over fifty years, my beloved Ursula.

In those days, the Jews in Germany were cut off from all community and social services, including but certainly not limited to the so-called Winter Relief Effort. They had to take care of themselves and organize their own campaigns.

During summer, volunteers visited Jewish houses, asking for clothing and any other household articles the Jewish families could spare to give to the poor. One Sunday the relief workers came to our house, but no one was home, so they left a little note. The following day, a Monday, my mother asked me to take the package which she had prepared over to a family named Bohm, who lived across the street and acted as a sort of collecting agent for all the parcels the volunteers had gathered in our neighborhood. I complied with my mother's request, albeit reluctantly, as I had intended to cut classes at the university on that day and go swimming instead.

I went over to the apartment of the Bohms, where the lady of the house, Frau Edith Bohm, received me and engaged me in a pleasant conversation about my family and my relatives, whom she had known for many years. In the middle of the conversation, the door opened and a lovely blond girl of about sixteen years came in, obviously to find out with whom her mother was talking. She and I soon became engaged in a very animated conversation, which turned into a debate about Zionism and Revisionism, including my youth group, the Betar. Having been brought up in a liberal German-Jewish home, Ursula was rather critical of Zionism and of its endeavor to convert what was then Palestine into a Jewish homeland. Jewish nationalism did not appeal to her—not yet.

It turned out that Ursula had decided to cut classes at the Jewish Gymnasium on the same day in order to avoid a written test in mathematics for which she was not well prepared. What a lucky coincidence! Suffice it to say that I was quite impressed with and attracted to this beautiful young girl.

When I finally got up to leave, I asked Ursula whether we could see each other again "to continue the discussion." She said "okay," but without great enthusiasm. However, as so often in my life, I did not take "no" for an answer. So we met again, continued our discussion, went to the movies, and took bike rides together. I even coached Ursula in Hebrew to prepare for her tests at the Jewish Gymnasium, which she had entered after the principal of the public high school for girls had asked all of the Jewish students to leave. A few months after meeting Ursula I realized that I had fallen in love with her. However, it appeared that my feelings remained unrequited, at least for some time.

It was December 31, 1937. I telephoned Ursula and asked her to spend New Year's Eve with me. She declined, and when

I asked her what she was doing she said that she intended to spend New Year's Eve with her parents in a restaurant, the Cafe Fahrig, one of the few restaurants that were still accessible to Jews. I showed up there later in the evening. Ursula's father was rather reserved, while her mother was very friendly toward me and immediately invited me to sit at their table. I invited Ursula to dance. All of a sudden, I noticed that the invisible wall which had blocked any romantic relationship between us began to crumble. On the way home I asked Ursula for a date. She accepted. The next day we went to the movies, where we held hands.

Thus began our courtship; however, it took six months before we were secretly engaged. This happened in Berlin in July or early August 1938. Ursula and her mother were visiting Ursula's Aunt Hedel, and I stopped in Berlin for a few days on my way home from the Baltic. We met in a restaurant at a place named Schildhorn, located on one of the beautiful lakes of the Havel River near Berlin. I proposed to Ursula while we were walking through a forest surrounding the lake. Ursula consented on condition that we keep it a secret for the time being. When we returned to the restaurant where Ursula's mother and her aunt were waiting, we saw the headlines of the newspapers announcing that Mussolini had just proclaimed his decision to enact racial laws against Italian Jews.

After our return to Breslau we continued our courtship and discussed our future together, which at the time seemed rather nebulous. I was determined to leave Germany as soon as I could get a visa to someplace overseas, whereas Ursula, barely seventeen years old, wanted to complete her high school education and to pass the Abitur.

In early December 1938, after I had purchased a steamship ticket to Peru on a boat due to sail on December 24, we decided to break the news of our engagement to Ursula's parents and ask for their blessings. Since Ursula's mother had shown a great deal of understanding of our romance, unlike her father, who believed that Ursula was too young for any serious relationship, we decided to make her mother our secret "ally" in the hope that she would bring her husband around.

We told her that we wanted to formally announce our engagement on December 19, one day before my departure. On the afternoon of December 19 we went to a small jewelry store called Schmuckkaestchen (Jewelry Box) and selected engagement rings.

We would wear these rings for almost fifty-one years.

On the evening of December 19, I called on Ursula's parents to ask for their approval of our engagement. While Ursula's mother showed no hesitancy in giving her blessing, her husband's reaction was one of resignation. He answered, "I believe my daughter is still too young to be engaged. However, inasmuch as things have already progressed so far, I will join my wife."

When I left Germany the next day, Ursula and I did not know whether or when we would see each other again; however, she was able to leave Germany for England on the last crossing of the *Bremen* before the war, in August 1939. Half a year later she left England on a perilous transatlantic crossing through U-boat infested waters to join me as my wife in La Paz, Bolivia.

While I was pursuing my studies at Breslau University, Nazi oppression of the Jews in Germany became gradually worse. The humiliation and restrictions to which German Jews were subjected through a number of infamous decrees isolated them completely from public life, stigmatized them, and prevented them from earning a livelihood. These decrees made life utterly intolerable.

While millions of Germans cheered Hitler, who had torn up the Treaty of Versailles and promised the Germans their "rightful place in the sun," a number of dissenting voices could be heard, albeit in a very low tone. I remember in particular a philosophy seminar on Heidegger one winter afternoon in 1937. When the professor exalted the "superiority" of the Aryan race, for which he claimed there was "ample scientific evidence," a Protestant theology student stood up and objected to the doctrine of racism, which he claimed was "the resurrection of paganism and unacceptable to a Christian." After the seminar, he and I walked home. When I asked him why he had exposed himself to such obvious danger, he replied that his conscience did not permit him to just sit there and listen to such "revolting nonsense."

I was involved in a number of anti-Semitic incidents, one of which I remember very clearly. It occurred on a lake named Mueritzsee (Lake Mueritz), a beautiful resort in Mecklenburg, where I spent part of my summer vacation with a Jewish family from Liegnitz, near Breslau. I was swimming in the lake when suddenly a man with a large German shepherd dog appeared on the shore of the lake and asked if I was Jewish. When I answered that I was, he threatened to set the dog on me unless I got out of the water immediately.

In the summer of 1938 I decided to leave Germany. I went to Berlin and called on a large number of embassies of various overseas countries, such as the United States and the Latin American countries. This proved to be an exercise in futility, as almost every country had closed its borders to Jewish refugees. Through a travel agency in Berlin I learned that there was a possibility of obtaining a tourist visa to Peru through rather devious means. While the Peruvian consul in Germany refused to issue any visas, the Peruvian consul in Paris, France, was issuing a number of such visas, in exchange for a little "compensation." The catch was that the money had to be paid in U.S. dollars. It was strictly prohibited for any resident of Germany to possess any foreign currency in Germany or abroad. I started writing letters to friends and purported relatives abroad, including all the "Baers" listed in the New York City telephone directory, asking them for a "loan" in dollars to save my life, assuring them that I would pay them back as soon as I had found a job abroad. The few answers I received were all negative, except one from a very distant cousin who had emigrated to Gastonia, North Carolina. His mother lived in Breslau, and we made an arrangement whereby he would remit the sum of $280 to the Peruvian consul in Paris. In return, my mother would pay his mother the equivalent of $280 in German marks. All these plans took several months to work out, and the arrangements were not completed until early November 1938, when the tragic events of Kristallnacht, which should more appropriately be called "Pogrom Night," burst upon us.

On the gray morning of November 10, 1938, my family received a telephone call from friends informing us that our synagogue was on fire and that mobs were looting Jewish-owned stores. My father immediately left to go to his office. This was the last time I saw him. I took the streetcar to the synagogue and saw the huge structure with the beautiful dome engulfed in flames. Some of the passengers exclaimed, "Why don't they throw all the Jews into their synagogue?" On the way back I saw the destruction of Jewish stores, the broken glass covering the sidewalk and people carrying away merchandise. While walking toward our house, I ran into my sister's husband, who told me that a lot of people were being arrested and that the two of us should at least try to escape to Berlin, where we might have a better chance of "going underground." We immediately packed some of our belongings. I tried to telephone my father at his office but was unable to reach him. My mother urged us to leave at once. She wanted to stay in order to help my father escape. Before leaving Breslau I quickly went to the Bohms' apartment in order to warn them and to ask Ursula's father to leave at once. I still remember this rather short man pulling himself up to his full height and saying to me, "I was a German soldier decorated with the Iron Cross—nothing will happen to me." Fortunately, as I learned later, he finally gave in to his wife's entreaties and was able to escape to Berlin.

On the way to the railroad station we encountered a group of Jewish men driven by SS guards and surrounded by a jeering mob. Like thousands of other Jews throughout Germany, they had been arrested by the Gestapo and were being driven to the railroad station, where they were herded into trains which would take them to various concentration camps throughout Germany.

We boarded the train to Berlin, where we arrived four hours later. In order to escape arrest and deportation we went to a movie house playing *Bengali*. Afterwards we walked down the Kurfuerstendamm and soon noticed a huge heap of glimmering ashes, which was all that remained of the beautiful temple on Fasanenstrasse. In front of the ruins I saw an old man leaning on a cane. He shook his head and exclaimed "What a shame for Germany."

I had two relatives in Berlin, one a widowed aunt, my grandfather's sister, Tante Rosa, who lived in the suburb of Spandau, and another aunt who lived on Wilhelmstrasse. I decided to stay with my aunt at Wilhelmstrasse. As soon as I arrived at her apartment we tried to reach my mother in Breslau in order to find out what had happened to my father and the rest of the family. My mother informed me that my father was in "police custody" and that they had heard nothing from him. As I would find out after my return to Breslau, two SS guards had come to our apartment shortly after I left in order to arrest my father and me. They told my mother that unless both of us presented ourselves to the police without delay, our home would be demolished. When my dad came home, he decided to give himself up to the police and went to the police precinct. Upon leaving he said to my mother "after all I have done nothing wrong, and I don't want you to be harassed." A few days later my aunt who lived in Spandau, near Berlin, called and asked me to see her right away. When I arrived at her home she said that I would have to summon up all of my strength in order to be able to face the news she had to give me. She then told me that she had just received a telephone call from my sister, who had informed her that the Gestapo had called my mother and told her that my father had died of a heart attack in the concentration camp at Buchenwald.

I was unable to comprehend what had happened. I was in a daze for several days. A few days later the newspaper announced that Goebbels had called off the "spontaneous outburst of the populace against the Jews" *(Kohende Volksseele)* and that no further arrests would be made. At the same time it was announced that the government would compel the Jewish community in Germany to pay "Jews' Penance" *(Judenbusse)* of several billion Reichsmark for the "tragedy" which they had inflicted on Germany as well as in payment of the clean-up costs caused by the destruction of Jewish property resulting from the "public outcry" against the Jews. I decided to wait another few days before returning to Breslau. We were met by my sister on the platform of the railroad station. My sister informed me that in my absence she had applied for a passport on my behalf so that I could leave Germany as soon as possible. My mother told me that a week before our return she was summoned to the Gestapo headquarters. When she arrived there, she was informed that my father had suffered a fatal heart attack while in "protective custody" at Buchenwald. They then handed my mother a cardboard box containing my father's ashes. When my mother cried out, they told her not to carry on and to leave. A few days after our arrival in Breslau, my father's ashes were deposited at the Jewish cemetery on Lohestrasse, where my mother's parents are buried.

As I found out later from friends who were interned at Buchenwald together with my father, he collapsed from exhaustion at the entrance to the concentration camp and was mercilessly beaten by SS guards.

When I returned home about two weeks after going into hiding in Berlin, I found a letter from the president of Breslau University. Although this letter, together with other personal papers, was lost with part of my baggage in transit from South America to the United States in 1945, I still remember the first paragraph. It read as follows:

> In order to prevent unpleasant incidents, I hereby forbid you to enter the campus of this University. *(Um Unzutraeglichkeiten zu vermeiden, untersage ich Ihnen das Betreten der Universitaet.)*

Before the November days of 1938 many of us German Jews still harbored the illusion that despite Nazi oppression our physical existence was not in danger. This illusion was rooted in the belief that the civilized world would not tolerate such outbursts. After the events of November 9, this illusion was shattered like the broken glass of Kristallnacht.

In order to enable me to find a job after leaving Germany, I tried to obtain character references from four of my former professors. One, who had meanwhile moved to Berlin, did not answer my request. Another, who lived a few blocks from us and whom I tried to see, did not let me into his flat but talked to me in the stairwell and declined my request. The third asked me for a "fee" of twenty Deutschmark. The fourth, my former professor of *Kulturgeschichte* (history of culture) not only gave me an excellent letter of recommendation but added the following line, "I should be very happy to hear how you are doing."

When I went to the central police station to pick up my passport, the official, an elderly man, handed me my passport with the words, "You are very fortunate, being able to leave Germany at this time. Who knows what's in store for us Germans under this regime?" He added that he belonged to the Bibelforscher group (Jehovah's Witnesses). He shook hands with me and wished me good luck.

In the meantime, I had booked passage on a Chilean vessel, the *Imperial,* to take me to Peru from Hamburg, Germany. I was to sail on December 24, 1938. Before leaving Germany, I telephoned my good friend Fritz Pasch, with whom I had grown up and who had left a few years before for Holland, where he was working for Phillips in Eindhoven. He suggested that instead of embarking in Hamburg, I take the ship at Antwerp, Belgium, which was to be first port of call and where he would take me by car after my visit to him over the Christmas holidays. Accordingly, I made arrangements for train travel from Breslau to Amsterdam via Berlin.

On December 20, 1938, an extremely cold day, I was taken to the railroad station in Breslau by my mother, Ursula, and my Uncle Gerson, who had come from Upper Silesia to say goodbye to me. I was overwhelmed by a feeling of despair as I waved at them out of the window of the moving train, not knowing whether I would ever see any of them again. About three and one half hours later I arrived in Berlin, where I called upon the Dutch embassy in order to obtain a transit visa for Holland. The official at the embassy told me that I did not need a transit visa, since I was in possession of an overseas visa and a steamship ticket.

At eleven o'clock that night I took the express train from Berlin to Amsterdam. I gave a sigh of relief after we crossed the Dutch border. A few minutes later, the train stopped at Oldenzaal, Holland, where Dutch customs officials inspected our passports. They returned mine and told me that I could not be admitted to Holland because I did not have a transit visa. When I replied that I had been advised by the Dutch embassy in Berlin the day before that I did not need one, the officials said that a new regulation requiring transit visas had just been issued by the Dutch government one hour before. They shipped me back to Osnabrueck, Germany, into the waiting arms of the Gestapo. The Gestapo told me that I was about to be taken to a concentration camp; however, by pointing out to them that I had a steamship ticket and would leave Germany within three days, I was able to persuade them to let me go.

I took the night train to Hamburg, where I was met by my cousin Peter Block (now in Toronto), who was waiting for his British visa to permit him to join his father in London.

C · h · a · p · t · e · r   T · h · r · e · e

PERU

I SAILED FROM HAMBURG on December 24, 1938, with a group of refugees bound for Peru, Bolivia, and Chile. In Antwerp, Belgium, another group of refugees came aboard. There was one complication: our Peruvian tourist visas were "irregular," as they should have been issued by the Peruvian consul in Germany, where we were residents, and not by the Peruvian consul in Paris, France. Our visas therefore required us to land at Mollendo, a small port in the south of Peru, and not in Callao, Peru's principal port, near Lima, where immigration officials were more likely to detect the irregularity of our visas. One of the passengers who boarded the ship in Antwerp, and who, thirty-five years later, was to become my nephew Michael Gluecksman's music teacher in Australia, went to see the Peruvian consul in Antwerp and asked the consul to change his port of disembarkation from Mollendo to Callao.

A few hours later, a little man in a bowler hat appeared on board the ship. He introduced himself as the Peruvian consul. He told the captain in the presence of the passengers that all of our visas were null and void. He demanded that the captain return us to Hamburg and threatened that, unless the captain complied with his wishes, he would report the matter to his government in Lima, which would not permit us to land. The captain refused this demand in very earthy language. He told the consul that he would take no orders from him and that it was his duty to take the passengers, all of whom had paid for their steamship tickets, to their destination. The captain then ordered the Peruvian consul off the ship.

It goes without saying that all the passengers were furious at this fellow passenger and were almost ready to cast him overboard. The passengers formed a committee in order to deal with this situation and, since I already spoke English, they asked me to head the committee. We decided to wire the Jewish Refugee Committee in New York and ask them to intervene with the Peruvian authorities so we could land in Peru.

The next day we put to sea and sailed through the English Channel toward the Atlantic. Our sense of relief at escaping the hell of Nazi Germany was overshadowed by our doubts as to whether or not we would be permitted to land in Peru. I will never forget the Shabbat services on board the ship, conducted by a young rabbi, Manfred Lubliner, from Upper Silesia, who was bound for Chile. We attended the services with heavy hearts, as we were faced with an uncertain destiny in a new and unknown country even if we succeeded in landing there. Somehow we shared the feelings of the Israelites on their way to the desert after their liberation from Egyptian slavery.

These thoughts were certainly not alleviated by the seasickness that overcame many of us in the North Atlantic, including me. The sea was extremely rough and tossed the five-thousand-ton vessel, which sailed entirely on ballast, like a nutshell. We were thrown from one side to the other of our bunk beds. My daily diet on the boat consisted entirely of *Zwieback* and tea.

I shared my cabin with two other passengers, one originally from Poland, who had been a stockbroker in Berlin, and the other named Henry Meyersfeld, from Braunschweig, with whom I was to establish a long-lasting friendship.

After twelve days on the ocean we sighted land. It was Chesapeake Bay. Columbus and his sailors could not have been more elated than we were, when they discovered the

New World. A few hours later we docked at Baltimore, Maryland, where we were met by representatives of the Jewish Relief Committee and reporters from the Baltimore press, as the news of the arrival of the first refugee boat from Europe had preceded us.

Since I was the only passenger who spoke English fluently (although, as a *Baltimore Sun* reporter put it, "like a Britisher"), I became the passengers' spokesperson and was interviewed by news reporters.

It felt wonderful to have *terra firma* under our feet after the twelve-day nightmare in the stormy North Atlantic.

One of the *Baltimore Sun* reporters drove me around Baltimore. I was quite impressed by the campus of Johns Hopkins University, with acres of parked cars. It was hard for me to believe that these cars belonged to students, since in Europe the average student was very fortunate if he or she owned a bicycle.

The same reporter took me to a fabulous dinner at the Lord Baltimore Hotel. He wanted to hear from me about the atrocities committed by the Nazis in Germany. However, I had to be very cautious not to jeopardize the safety of my family, whom I had left behind.

In order to illustrate the fact that the United States allows complete freedom of expression, my host, the news reporter, jumped on the table (after a few drinks) and shouted "President Roosevelt is a God-damned fool." I was scared stiff, as I thought that at any time the secret police would haul him away. However, nothing of the kind happened. Instead, the people around us started laughing, and some of them even clapped in agreement.

Two couples seated at a neighboring table drew me into an animated conversation. One couple introduced themselves as "the Simons" and the other as "the Schusters." They added that they were running a publishing house in New York (Simon & Schuster) and were now on their way to Florida.

A summary of the interview I gave appeared subsequently in the *Baltimore Sun*. The description of Nazi oppression of the Jews, specifically of the November 1938 pogrom, was understated and did not indicate my name. I had told the reporter that a realistic portrayal stating my name might jeopardize my family's safety. During her visit to Baltimore in 1990, my daughter Gabriela obtained from the public library a copy of the edition of the *Baltimore Sun* in which my interview appeared. The article was entitled "German Refugees Stop in City on Way to South America."

During this four-day visit to Baltimore we were befriended by representatives of the Baltimore Jewish community. I had my first experience with a typical Jewish-American delicatessen. There I met a young man by the name of Sam Lessing, owner of a local store that sold Westinghouse products. He promised to sponsor my immigration to the United States from South America by furnishing me with an Affidavit of Support. He kept his promise; however, the American consul in La Paz, Bolivia, to whom I presented the affidavit, turned me down on the ground that the "insufficiency" of my sponsor's resources created the danger to the United States that I might become "a public charge."

A few people I met in Baltimore suggested that, since it was difficult to immigrate legally to the United States, I should "just get lost" in Baltimore and take any kind of job that I might find. But I thought it better to continue to South American as planned.

A few days later we sailed for our next port of call, New York, where the U.S. immigration officials did not permit us to go ashore. They were apprehensive that we might prefer the United States to Peru. The only exception they made was for a young girl with acute appendicitis, who was carried from the ship on a stretcher and taken to an emergency hospital in New York.

The Statue of Liberty, which slowly emerged from the early morning mist hovering over the entrance to New York Harbor, made an unforgettable impression on all of us who had just escaped the murderous clutches of the Nazis.

As soon as the boat docked, several representatives of various Jewish committees, having heard of the threats made by the Peruvian consul in Antwerp, came aboard to discuss our visa problems. We were assured that these committees had appealed to several influential American humanitarians, including Eleanor Roosevelt, requesting their intervention with Peruvian authorities, and that they had sent a delegate to Lima to "negotiate" with the Peruvian government. We later discovered that effective "negotiations" with South American authorities usually involve certain financial "accommodations."

I had been almost completely penniless when I boarded the ship in Hamburg. During our Atlantic crossing I was able to earn a small amount of money by giving Spanish lessons to first-class passengers.

A day or two after docking in New York harbor, we continued our voyage and passed through the Panama Canal. I remember my amazement in Panama City, Cristobal, and Balboa when I noticed shop signs bearing names such as "Mizraji," "Diez de Medina," and others of obviously Jewish origin. The bearers of these names were descendants of Spanish Jews, who had fled from Spain to escape the Inquisition.

After leaving the Panama Canal and reaching the calm Pacific, we stopped at several seaports in Ecuador and northern Peru. A few days later we reached the Port of Callao, where immigration officials told us that we were not permitted to land in Peru, since we had irregular visas. This, of course, did not exactly help to boost our morale. Subsequently, representatives of the Jewish Refugee Aid Committee in Lima visited us onboard the ship and told us arrangements had been made with the port authorities of Mollendo, the southern port of Peru, who would permit us to land there. Shortly thereafter we reached Mollendo. We anchored in the open sea, as Mollendo did not have any docking facilities for oceangoing ships. Our boat was approached by small launches manned by characters who bore striking resemblances to the Pirates of the Caribbean at Disneyland, which I visited many years later.

When we approached the shore after a rough ride on these boats, the port workers dropped chairs fastened by ropes into the boats. Each of the passengers was tied to a chair, which was then hoisted by some primitive mechanism in order to drop its human cargo unceremoniously on the docks.

As soon as we cleared customs we were approached by a number of individuals who asked us whether we had American cigarettes, whisky, cameras, or other valuable articles to sell. My friend Meyersfeld and I checked into a small hotel named Gran Hotel.

In the middle of the night we woke up and started scratching. Ever since, the word *pulga* (flea) has been indelibly etched in my memory. We left the hotel around midnight and spent the rest of the night on benches on the Plaza de Armas, a park lined by palm trees. The local gendarme, on his beat, undoubtedly wondered what these gringos were up to.

The Jewish Committee in Lima, which had visited us on our boat in Callao, had told us to take the train from Mollendo to Arequipa, the second-largest city in Peru, where they would help us get settled. We wanted to take the ten o'clock train the next morning, and were about to board it when we were stopped by a police officer. He told us that we were in violation of a purported law which required immigrants passing through the port of Mollendo to take the next available train to their destination. He added that the "next train" had left at six o'clock the prior evening. He sternly demanded a certain amount of money as a "fine" in order, as he put it, to protect his "responsibility." However, the amount of the "fine" proved to be a highly negotiable figure.

After paying the "fine" we boarded the train. Within a few hours it climbed from sea level to an altitude of approximately 8,300 feet and was surrounded by scenery that can only be compared to a moonscape. In Arequipa we were met by a delegate of the Lima Jewish Committee, who put us up in a little hotel.

The City of Arequipa, founded by Spaniards in the seventeenth century and situated at the foot of an extinct volcano named Misti, was impressive with its white buildings and beautiful cathedral, designed by a French architect. It had an excellent climate.

The day after our arrival I went hunting for a job as an

English-Spanish commercial correspondent. On my fifth day in Arequipa I had an interview with an international trading company and steamship agency, Enrique W. Gibson & Co. Ltd., owned by a London firm and by the former vice-president of Peru and dean of Arequipa University, Don Enrique Gibson. I was interviewed by Don Enrique, who took a liking to me and told me that his firm would employ me as assistant correspondent in English and Spanish. He added that, in view of my academic background, he would want me to teach a course in philosophy at the university. Unfortunately, it turned out that the *recursos financieros* (financial resources) for this position were not available.

When I informed him that I had a visa problem, he told me not to worry, since, as former vice-president of Peru, he had a great deal of influence. He added that he would ask the foreign minister of Peru to "legalize" me. He was true to his promise. I was employed by this firm, and the salary I earned permitted me to hold body and soul together and pay the rent for a modest apartment.

I learned a great deal about basic import and export procedures and accounting. I was placed in charge of keeping and watching the list of accounts receivable named *deudores morosos* ("dilatory debtors") also—not unrealistically—called "the *mañana* accounts." My daily office routine commenced at 9:00 A.M. I went home for lunch and siesta from 12:00 to 2:00 P.M., then returned to the office and stayed there until about 6:00 P.M. The afternoons were pleasantly interrupted by the office boy serving tea, coffee, and pastries. No one was overworked.

There were very few Jews in Arequipa. Most of them were merchants who had come from Romania and Poland. They kept their ethnic and religious backgrounds to themselves. One of them, Miguel Feldman, had a store on the Plaza de Armas. Since there was no synagogue in Arequipa, we held our Friday evening services in the back room of his store.

A few weeks after my arrival at Arequipa, my friend Meyersfeld and I went shopping for pots and pans on a Saturday morning. We entered one of the stores, and after we had told the shopkeeper what we wanted he asked us to wait a few minutes. It was close to one o'clock in the afternoon, and since everybody stopped working on Saturday at one o'clock, he soon rolled down the shutters and asked us to follow him to his living quarters in the rear of the store. We climbed a few steps and I noticed a huge crucifix over the entrance door. He showed us into the living room and, to our surprise, he said "*Yo tambien soy hijo de su pueblo*" (I am also a son of your people). He then proceeded to open a sideboard and, to our further astonishment, took out a small Sefer Torah (scroll of the Bible). He told us that his ancestors had fled the Spanish Inquisition and had immigrated to South America several centuries ago. Though they had outwardly converted to Catholicism, they as well as all of their descendants, including himself, had instructed their children in the Torah and in Jewish traditions, although no one else knew about it. He pointed out that this year he had been selected to carry the crucifix at the head of the Easter procession. He asked us to keep in touch with him and to see him whenever we needed advice. Suffice it to say that we got our pots and pans at bargain prices.

Arequipa was a lovely medium-sized city with typically Spanish customs. The center of social activity was the Plaza de Armas. Every Sunday morning after church services, boys and girls would parade up and down the Plaza de Armas. The girls in their Sunday best would walk in one direction, the boys in the opposite direction, and furtive glances would be exchanged. A few times a year a traveling Spanish opera company performed Spanish operas called *zarzuelas*. These were the outstanding cultural and social events of the year.

Under the archway that lined the Plaza de Armas, Quechua women, descendants of the Incas, sold fruit and vegetables. Several times each week I went there to buy fruit. The ritual consisted of the Indian woman naming a price, which was followed by my counter-offer. After a few minutes a deal was struck. Everybody was happy, having saved their *dignidad* (face), and I was on my way home.

The Catholic Church had seen to it that prejudice against the Jews was kept alive. Although most of the local people I met were helpful and interested in our background, I was told that we couldn't possibly be Jews since we didn't have horns. None of them had ever seen a Jew before.

A few weeks after our arrival, the local Catholic paper, *El Deber*, published an article in which they deplored the arrival of "a large number of Jews" who had been expelled from Europe for their "misdeeds" and the harm they had inflicted upon their communities. Although this article did not have any serious consequences, it did not help our relations with the community.

$C \cdot h \cdot a \cdot p \cdot t \cdot e \cdot r \quad F \cdot o \cdot u \cdot r$

BOLIVIA

DURING THE MONTHS following my arrival in Arequipa, the situation of the Jews in Germany deteriorated rapidly. It was now mid-1939, and everyone expected the outbreak of war at any moment. I was doing my best to try to help my mother, Ursula, and her parents to obtain Peruvian visas. However, this was impossible or, to put it in more realistic terms, unaffordable.

In the meantime, I learned that visas to Bolivia, a neighboring country, separated from Peru by Lake Titicaca, were still available and affordable. I requested the honorary consul of Bolivia in Arequipa to issue Bolivian visas to my mother, Ursula, and her parents. Though he was at first quite reluctant to do so, I finally succeeded in persuading him to stamp Bolivian visas into their passports, which they had airmailed to me. The passports were returned to my family in Germany. Unfortunately, in the meantime, all steamship companies had been instructed to sell steamship tickets to overseas passengers only if visas had been issued by the consuls in the applicants' respective countries. This of course invalidated the visas that I had obtained at substantial cost.

Since Bolivian visas were still obtainable in La Paz, I decided to take immediate action. I pulled up stakes in Peru and within a few days was on board the train that took me up to

Puno, the Peruvian border station on Lake Titicaca, the highest lake in the world (approximately 13,000 feet), not too far from Cuzco, the ancient capital of Peru.

After crossing Lake Titicaca by night, I arrived on the Bolivian side and took the train over the Altiplano (high plateau) to La Paz, located in a basin surrounded by towering mountains, at an altitude of over 3,600 meters (approximately 12,000 feet). The air is extremely thin due to the altitude, and most Europeans and Americans were having a tough time getting used to it. At the La Paz railroad station I was met by Ursula's Uncle Edwin and his wife, Adele, as well as by my school friend, Rabbi Helmut Gins—all of whom had recently arrived from Germany. I rented a room in the house in which Edwin and Adele lived. A wave of immigrants from Germany, Austria, and Czechoslovakia had recently arrived in the two principal cities of Bolivia, La Paz and Cochabamba. They found it extremely difficult to get settled. The culture shock and the climatic as well as linguistic difficulties they experienced were compounded by their inability to engage in the occupations and professions they had practiced in Europe or to find other employment. Therefore, during the initial period following their immigration to Bolivia, most Jewish immigrants depended on the financial aid dispensed by the Jewish Relief Committee, which, in turn, was subsidized by the "Joint," an immigrant aid organization in the United States.

After a short time, I found a job as interpreter for the General Staff of the Bolivian Army, where I translated German and French military manuals into Spanish. After several weeks had elapsed without a paycheck, I approached my supervising officer, who assured me that I would be paid "mañana." A few days later he told me sheepishly that "through an inadvertence" no appropriation had been provided for the services of a translator in the Army's *presupuesto* (budget), and that he had been misinformed when hiring me. So much for my work for the Bolivian army as a "volunteer."

In the meantime, I tried to find a way to obtain visas for my mother and for Ursula's parents. This was complicated by the fact that war had meanwhile broken out in Europe. I found out that visas could be secured at a price through middlemen who had contacts with the Minister of Immigration and his staff. Since I spoke Spanish, I had the "guts" to seek an audience with the President of Bolivia, General Quintanilla. He had just taken over the reins of government from President Busch, who had died under mysterious circumstances. The audience had been arranged by my landlady's son, who knew an officer of the president's palace guard. I told the president that I had "volunteered" my services to the Bolivian army as a linguist, and that I intended to continue serving my "new fatherland" in the future, but that I needed to be reunited with my family. Within a few minutes the general called his *ayudante* and ordered him to send a cable to the Bolivian consul in Hamburg, Germany, with instructions to issue the visas for my mother and prospective in-laws.

The next thing I tried to accomplish was to get a visa for Ursula so that we could be married in Bolivia. However, this was not possible under Bolivian law, which prohibited the immigration of "unattached females" traveling without escort, an unusual "aberration" into morality. An imaginative lawyer, Señor Dr. Trigo, found a way. Since Bolivia permitted marriage by proxy (*por poder* or "by power of attorney"), he prepared the necessary power of attorney to be sent to Ursula in London. Ursula would have to sign it before the Bolivian consul. By virtue of said power, Ursula would appoint an attorney-in-fact in Bolivia to appear in her stead before a notary public in order to sign the civil marriage contract. The attorney-in-fact designated by Ursula would be her Aunt Adele, then a resident of La Paz. The power of attorney was prepared and forwarded to London. It was returned to me sealed and signed by Ursula a few weeks later. Adele and I appeared before the notary public, Rene Bueno. I said to the notary, *"Señor Notario, quisiera casarme por poder"* (Mr. Notary, I wish to get married by proxy). His reply was *"Mi amigo, hasta ahora nadie se ha casado por no poder."* This answer was a play on words and is untranslatable.

I forwarded the marriage certificate based on the power

of attorney to Ursula, who obtained her Chilean transit visa and her Bolivian immigration visa, as Bolivia, a land-locked country, can be reached from the Pacific coast only by way of Peru or Chile. Ursula and I were happily reunited in Bolivia on November 19, 1939. Her crossing of the North Atlantic from Liverpool, England, was extremely perilous, as the Atlantic was infested by German U-boats, which sank a large number of vessels, including one of the convoy ships escorting the *Orduña*, on which Ursula was a passenger.

Though we were happy to be together, we faced rough times, since it was very difficult for me to find a job. Therefore, I opened up an office as a freelance translator-interpreter. This did not bring in much money, although the Jewish Community used my services frequently, particularly when immigrants had legal problems. I remember several times when we shared an orange for lunch. However, we were young and confident that better times lay ahead. Our greatest concern was to help our parents book passage to Bolivia.

In this endeavor we had to face new obstacles. The Bolivian Ministry of Immigration had decreed that all visas that had already been granted required "ratification" by the government. Since Bolivian officials, like most South Americans, were known to be courteous and accommodating to ladies, Ursula and another lady whose parents were also still in Germany sought an audience with the Deputy Minister of Immigration. From among the many petitioners seeking ratification of their relatives' visas, Ursula and the lady accompanying her were the only ones whose petitions were granted. In the subsequent account of her conversation with the highest official of the Ministry of Immigration next to the Minister himself, Ursula said that at first he turned a deaf ear to her plea and tried to cut her off with the statement "*No somos salvavidas*" (We are no life-savers). Since the official's name was Johnson, it then occurred to Ursula to ask him whether his ancestors had come from Great Britain. When he answered in the affirmative and stated that he had studied in London, Ursula told him that she had just arrived from England, and that she had grown very fond of the English people, who had given her shelter upon her arrival as a refugee from Germany. This broke the ice, and the official agreed to grant visas to Ursula's parents, my mother, and to the other lady's parents. The official added the following warning: "If I hear that either one of you has mentioned anything about this decision to anybody else, I shall revoke the visas immediately."

Subsequently, Ursula's parents and my mother booked steamship tickets on an Italian vessel due to sail from Genova, Italy, to Arica, Chile, in June 1940. However, after Italy's entry into the war in May 1940, all shipping from Europe to South America ceased, and a new route had to be found. In August 1940, pursuant to arrangements made by the Jewish Committee, our parents traveled by train from Berlin, via Moscow, to Vladivostok by Trans-Siberian Railroad. From Vladivostok they were ferried to Pusan, Korea, then to Shimonoseki, Japan, and a few days later departed from Kobe, Japan, via Honolulu and Los Angeles, to Arica, Chile. In Arica they took the train to La Paz. The entire trip from Berlin to Bolivia took almost three months, and was fraught with dangers and hardships. We were overjoyed when we met them at the La Paz railroad station in November 1940. We all lived together in a little cottage in the midst of an eucalyptus grove. The primitive bathroom facilities were outside. Life was hard, but we were happy to be together.

Meanwhile, I found employment as an English-Spanish correspondent with a prominent import-export firm. A few months later, a friend of mine, a high official of the Bolivian Ministry of Agriculture, Señor Avila, offered me additional employment as interpreter-translator. When I told him that I could not see my way clear to handling two jobs at the same time, he smiled and said this presented no problem in Bolivia. He explained that nobody at the Ministry of Agriculture worked too hard, and he was sure that I, as a European, would accomplish in two to three hours in the evening what his employees were unable to complete during their eight-hour day. He turned out to be absolutely correct. I accepted this second employment, signed in every morning shortly before nine o'clock, and picked up the work to be done which consisted of articles to be translated; since the import-export company's offices were located just two blocks from the Ministry of Agriculture I was there punctually at nine o'clock. In the evening I completed the translations, and turned them in the next morning. Whenever I was needed during the day, which was not very often, my friend called me and I appeared within a matter of five minutes.

And so it went for quite some time until one day my "sponsor," Señor Avila, had an argument with the top executive of the Ministry of Agriculture—an argument of which both he and I were the casualties.

Although Bolivia was far away from the European continent, the war raging in Europe, even before Pearl Harbor, had its repercussions in that country. A large part of the Bolivian population, as well as the people in most South American countries, were very friendly toward the Germans. German businessmen had established themselves in Bolivia many years before World War II, and a German general had trained the Bolivian Army in preparation for the so-called "Chaco War" with Paraguay in the early 1930s.

Before and during World War II, the Nazis unleashed a very intensive propaganda campaign in Bolivia. Several influential persons in the media, obviously paid by the Nazis and taking advantage of the traditional resentment of the population against the *Imperialismo yanqui*, sympathized with the Nazi cause. On the other side of the political spectrum, shortly after the outbreak of the European war in 1939, a group of European refugees, Jewish and non-Jewish, banded together in order to fight the activities of the Nazis in Bolivia, through broadcasts, leaflets, and newspaper articles. The leader of this group was a non-Jewish refugee from Germany named Karl Schumacher, who had been active in the former German Social Democratic Party. He was the editor of an anti-Nazi paper published in the German language in La Paz. I was very active in this group, and published several anti-Nazi articles in the local press. This was very well known to the local

Nazis, whose center of activities was the German embassy. One day, as I was walking down the street with Ursula, an automobile from the German embassy stopped in front of us. Out jumped the chauffeur, who ran toward me in order to attack me. At that moment Ursula, who always had a fantastic presence of mind, stepped behind the chauffeur, and was about to hit him over the head with her umbrella. When the "brave" Nazi realized his predicament, he ran back toward his car and drove off.

During the second half of 1941, our group heard from confidential sources that a group of Bolivian army officers, supported by the Nazis in Bolivia, intended to stage a revolution to overthrow the Bolivian government and to install a new administration that would cooperate with the Axis powers. Although Bolivia was a small country, it was rich in strategic materials coveted by the Nazis, such as tin, tungsten, and other metals and minerals.

Our group conveyed these reports to the Bolivian government as well as to the embassies of Great Britain and the United States. However, we were advised that the embassies were unable to induce the Bolivian government to take any action without actual evidence of these activities. Accordingly, our group, which had connections with certain officials of the Bolivian Postal Administration, made "suitable arrangements" with those officials to "loan" to us, before delivery to the respective addressees, correspondence between Bolivian individuals, mostly military officials, and certain German sources, including officials of the German embassy suspected by us of carrying on these activities. Copies of this correspondence were sent to the Allied embassies. The contents substantiated the reports we had previously received and implicated the German embassy in a plot to "destabilize" the Bolivian government. As a result, in late 1941 Bolivia broke off diplomatic relations with Germany.

In addition, other kinds of problems had to be addressed. There were no satisfactory trade schools in La Paz for the occupational training of children of Jewish refugees from cen-

tral Europe, who had increased the previous Jewish population of only a few hundred families to several thousand
people within the short span of approximately three years,
and were without any pre-existing cultural or educational infrastructure.

Accordingly, several refugees, including me, who had
been teachers in the old country as well as those who had spe-
cialized knowledge in various technical areas, formed a Bolivian chapter of the ORT School, an international Jewish trade
school system, for the education and training of the young
generation. We volunteered our services during several late afternoons each week. I conducted courses in Spanish and English commercial correspondence and business practice. It
was most satisfying to be able to make at least a small contribution to the practical education of our fellow immigrants'
children in their new country. A few years ago, I ran into a
former student of mine, now a retired certified public accoun-
tant in the San Fernando Valley.

On January 1, 1942, Ursula and I had our first child, our
daughter Gabriela Esther. She was given her middle name,
Esther, in memory of Ursula's maternal grandmother. I took
Ursula to the American clinic in Obrajes, about fifteen miles
from La Paz. Most taxi drivers were drunk, as it was New Year's
Eve. I finally succeeded in getting a sober cab driver, a
"landsman" from my hometown, Breslau, who took Ursula,
me, and her parents safely to the clinic. Ursula's room was
next to that of a concubine of the president of Bolivia, who
gave birth at about the same time.

Ursula nursed Gaby for a long time, about eight or nine
months. She was a delightful baby, except that we had to use
all sorts of tricks to make her eat.

Since we spoke German at home, Gaby's first language
was German. She was three years old when we left Bolivia for
the United States and had not learned one word of Spanish.
Subsequently, when she attended kindergarten in Los Angeles, the other children called her "that little girl with the German accent." While Gaby learned to speak German as her

mother tongue, she was introduced to the beautiful melodies of Franz Lehar's and Emerich Kalman's operettas during her infancy. Ursula's father, who had been a stagehand at a theater in his native city of Beuthen, Upper Silesia, was familiar with operas and operettas. I can still see him carrying Gaby in his arm singing "Mein Herr Marquis" from *Die Fledermaus* and "Wer uns getraut" from *Der Zigeunerbaron*.

On the professional front, I endeavored to expand my practice as interpreter-translator. Most of my work consisted of services to refugees whose knowledge of Spanish was either deficient or non-existent. The Jewish Aid Committee, which gave financial assistance to the immigrants, also used my services. I remember one rather colorful case involving a criminal trial in which an immigrant had been charged with falsifying part of a cable addressed by the Bolivian Ministry of Immigration to the Bolivian Consul General in Hamburg, Germany, authorizing him to issue visas to certain Jewish families in Germany. The accused, a fellow by the name of Sittenfeld from Upper Silesia, was in very close touch with officials of the Ministry of Immigration and acted as intermediary between the Ministry and Jewish immigrants in connection with visa applications for these immigrants' relatives who were still in Germany. Since the government officials expected to be paid for these visa approvals, Sittenfeld collected the required amounts from the immigrants in Bolivia and added his own "fee." Upon approval of the visa petitions, the ministry would hand Sittenfeld the respective cable messages addressed to the Consul General in Hamburg. Sittenfeld, in turn, would go to the cable office and pay for the transmission of these messages.

One day, Sittenfeld had a "brilliant" idea. He used the empty space remaining at the bottom of one of the cablegrams and added a few more names. But he made the mistake of pocketing the entire amount he had received from the petitioners for these additional persons without sharing it with the immigration officials.

A few months later, the immigrants whose names had

been added to the cable arrived in La Paz. Upon verification of their names in the ministry's records by officials of the Ministry of Immigration, Sittenfeld's doctoring of the cable was discovered.

Sittenfeld was indicted, tried, and convicted. One of the co-defendants was a fellow by the name of Jacoby, an elderly immigrant from Berlin. He stuttered and was hard of hearing. On top of that, he was sort of a *schlemiel.* He had been given a cable by Sittenfeld to take to the cable office. I am sure he didn't know what was in the cable, since he didn't speak Spanish, the language in which the cable was written. He was the "fall guy," placed under arrest, put in a La Paz jail known as the *Panoptico,* in the San Pedro district, and charged with aiding and abetting a forgery.

The Jewish Aid Committee asked me to serve as Jacoby's interpreter and to maintain liaison with the public defender. I was appalled by the incompetence of Jacoby's counsel. During one of the conferences in the judge's chambers (there was no jury), I pointed out the many weaknesses of the prosecution's case against Jacoby. They had failed to introduce any evidence indicating that Jacoby, a poorly paid messenger, was aware of the forgery. The judge shrugged and told me that it was the defense counsel's responsibility to argue this point. Jacoby was convicted and sentenced to a prison term.

The Committee asked me to visit Jacoby after he had been sentenced, to make sure that he would receive decent treatment in jail. One morning, as I checked in at the prison, the warden asked me whether I knew Jacoby's whereabouts. He and Sittenfeld had escaped from prison during the night. I told the warden that I didn't even know that they had escaped. He responded that he would have to hold me pending further investigation. Before I knew what was happening, I was under arrest with one policeman on my left and another on my right, and taken to the police prison. I protested to the warden that if I had known about the escape, I certainly would not have shown up, but to no avail.

As I was being marched across town to jail, I happened to run into the local representative of the *Aufbau,* a New York

German-Jewish paper. I asked him to immediately notify Ursula of my predicament and to bring me some food, as I was very hungry. The chief of police, who knew me, soon apologized for this ridiculous situation. He told me that he would not want me to be thrown into jail together with drunken Indians and prostitutes, and he let me stay in his office.

About two hours later, Ursula appeared with Federico, our landlady's son, who had been a schoolmate of the president of Bolivia's chief of cabinet. A few minutes later I was a free man. Ursula and I laughed about this experience for many years to come.

Just a footnote to the Sittenfeld affair: When the time comes for Sittenfeld to appear before his Maker (if this has not already occurred), I am sure that on the scales of justice his misdeeds will be far outweighed by the benefit he bestowed, albeit for the wrong reasons, on those immigrants whose lives were saved as a result of his forgery. He thus performed the highest *mitzvah,* or religious duty, namely *Pikuach Nefesh,* or saving human lives from the hell of the Holocaust.

One day in late 1940, I was offered a position with one of the leading Bolivian mining companies in the Beni, Bolivia's tropical area, at the suspiciously high salary of $500.00 per month. Further inquiry disclosed that the area was infested by yellow fever. Shortly thereafter, another of the three large mining companies, Hochschild, which belonged to Mauricio Hochschild, a Jewish entrepreneur from Frankfurt and one of the three "tin barons" of Bolivia, offered me a position as assistant to the administrator of a tin mine high up in the Andes, at an altitude of over 15,000 feet. This unfortunately meant a temporary separation from Ursula, who was already having a hard time with the climate of La Paz. However, we figured that if I worked there for only a few months we would be able not only to support both of us, but also to make some savings.

The area was named Colquiri and the only means of transportation to that godforsaken place was by truck over a rocky and narrow mountain road with a ravine of between 1,000 and 2,000 feet on one side. At the bottom of the ravine were a number of trucks whose ill-fated drivers had failed to negotiate the sharp curves of the mountain road.

The mining camp was perched on the ridge of a desolate mountain range devoid of any vegetation. The socio-economic structure of Bolivia, and of Peru, was well exemplified by the housing pattern of the camp. The Indians, who were the lowest stratum and who furnished the bulk of the mine workers, lived in miserable shacks that were not even fit for animals.

Next in the pecking order came the Cholos, people of mixed European and Indian blood, who made up most of the intermediate operating and clerical staff. Their accommodations, while still sub-standard from a European or American perspective, had at least some of the appearances of human habitation, such as windows, wooden floors, beds, and running water.

The top management positions were exclusively in the hands of Americans and Europeans, who were paid in U.S. dollars. Their accommodations, and my own, consisted of neat little buildings equipped with modern facilities, and stood out like small palaces against the miserable shacks that surrounded them.

The Indians, most of whom were afflicted by a host of lung diseases as a result of their daily work in the mines hundreds of feet below ground, were perpetually enslaved to the company through the so-called *pulperia* system. The company operated the sole general store, or pulperia, in the area. Since the miserable wages the Indian workers were paid did not enable them to feed their large families, they were constantly indebted to the company store, and thus lived in virtual servitude for the rest of their short lives. A similar fate among American coal miners is vividly described in the song "Sixteen Tons," which was popular in the United States many years ago.

I was employed as a management assistant. Housing was free, food was relatively cheap, and Colquiri was hundreds of miles from the nearest city. Therefore there was hardly any money to spend, and management personnel could save most of their salaries, except for those who were or became addicted to the bottle.

The social dynamite generated by the shameless exploitation of the lower classes in many Latin American countries ruled by a small upper crust exploded in later years and created radical movements organized by Castro, Che Guevara, and the leaders of the "Sendero Luminoso" throughout Peru, Bolivia, and other countries on the West Coast of South America.

My stay at the mining camp was of short duration. While I had experienced little difficulty with the climate of La Paz, at an altitude of approximately 3,600 meters (12,000 feet), I could not tolerate the tremendous altitude of Colquiri. I woke up each morning and gasped for breath. After a few weeks, the company physician urged me to leave without delay. I did so without regrets.

After my return to La Paz, I went job hunting for several months. Finally, through a good friend of ours, I landed a job as assistant to the import manager of a prominent local import-export firm. I was to take care of the correspondence in English and Spanish, mostly with suppliers in the United States and Great Britain, which the firm represented in Bolivia.

After approximately two years, another opportunity presented itself. The La Paz correspondent for UPI (United Press International), an American who was a friend of mine, told me that in view of the threat of Japanese invasion of Southeast Asia, which was a substantial source of raw materials such as rubber, metals, and minerals, the United States government was turning its attention to South American countries such as Bolivia and Peru as replacement sources for these vital raw materials. In this endeavor the United States needed the advice of politically reliable people who were familiar with the mentality and customs of these countries, had command of Spanish, and had knowledge of the socio-economic and political conditions of the area. My friend was convinced that I met these requirements, and since I was not a native of Bolivia, my judgment and advice would be objective. A few weeks later, my friend reported to me that the American ambassador wished to meet me. Accordingly, I went to the embassy for an interview with the ambassador, who hired me on the spot as economic advisor and interpreter-translator. Although my salary in the beginning was rather modest, it was paid in dollars, which, in light of the almost worthless Bolivian currency, was a great advantage.

After Pearl Harbor the section of the embassy for which I worked was named Board of Economic Warfare, BEW for short. Later on, toward the end of the war, the name was changed to Foreign Economic Administration, or FEA.

My responsibilities as economic analyst-advisor included a large number of activities. One of them was the investigation and identification of those business enterprises that continued trading with the enemy, that is, Germany, Italy, or Japan, directly or through third parties. Firms which were so identified were subsequently included in the so-called "Statutory List" or "blacklist" by the Allies, which resulted in their automatic exclusion from any business relationship with suppliers in Britain and the U.S. As Bolivia, like other South American countries, became increasingly dependent on the United States for basic goods and services (Bolivia imported practically everything), such exclusion from U.S. trade was a crippling blow to any firm. Bolivia was a landlocked country, and all of its imported goods had to be shipped through Peru, Chile, or Argentina. In view of their pro-Nazi and pro-fascist sympathies, a large number of Argentine enterprises and, of course, numerous German and Italian business firms that had been established in Argentina for many years were instrumental in camouflaging German or Italian goods that had been shipped to Buenos Aires (mostly on Spanish vessels), by changing the labels and markings showing the origin of the merchandise, which was subsequently shipped to Bolivia by rail.

In our efforts to identify such goods and the firms involved in these activities, we were aided by the commercial intelligence section of the American embassy in Buenos Aires as well as by businessmen, forwarding agents, customs brokers, and others sympathetic to the Allied cause.

As the Germans were interested in obtaining strategic materials produced by Bolivia, such as tin, tungsten, and other metals and minerals, our section had to keep a watchful eye on clandestine exportation of such materials from Bolivia to the Axis powers through Argentina and other South American countries, mostly on the Atlantic seaboard.

After Pearl Harbor, the United States economy converted to a war economy. This meant drastic restrictions of the production and consumption of U.S. goods and services for civilian purposes. It also meant severe cutbacks in the allocation of American products for export. This led to the introduction of the U.S. Export Licensing System, remnants of which, interestingly enough, are still in effect today as a result of the Cold War.

Pursuant to these regulations, every importer of American goods who placed an order with a U.S. supplier had to provide certification by the Commercial Office of the American embassy that the volume of goods to be imported reflected the company's "normal needs." This was done in order to prevent speculation and black-market prices for goods in short supply.

It was my responsibility to screen these export license applications.

Another very interesting area of my activity was of a political nature. It was the policy of the U.S. State Department to help maintain at least a degree of political "stability" in Bolivia and other Latin American countries in which the U.S. had strong economic interests. This meant support of a thin upper crust of less than five percent of the population, consisting mostly of land owners and "tin barons," who owned everything, while the rest of the population had nothing.

This unholy alliance between the U.S. government and the established order exacerbated the hostility of the population toward the perceived "*yanqui* oppressors."

One day the chief of our mission called me into his office

and informed me that he would entrust me with a very delicate and responsible assignment. He told me that he believed the State Department was being fed the wrong kind of information on political conditions in Bolivia by the ambassador's sole source of information, representatives of the ruling oligarchy, who of course told him that everything was well in Bolivia and that there was nothing to worry about. My chief, Mr. Kazen, added that his preliminary information indicated otherwise and that my assignment was to establish "discreet" contacts with some of the leading representatives of the lower classes of the population, such as labor union leaders who represented the mine workers and other trades. In addition, since it was well known that a large section of the military and the right-wing political parties were Nazi sympathizers, I should try to find out if there was any danger of the current regime, headed by General Enrique Peñaranda, a friend of the United States, being overthrown by "fellow officers." In this connection one should not forget that Bolivia has had more revolutions than any other country in South America, and that until that time no president had ever served out his term. My assignment was difficult but challenging.

I spoke with representatives of the labor unions and, not to my surprise, found out that there was widespread dissatisfaction with the miserable plight of the mine workers on account of low wages and intolerable working conditions. The workers blamed not only their immediate bosses, the "tin barons," but also the Americans, who, in the eyes of the workers, were the beneficiaries of their exploitation. On the other side of the political spectrum were the military, particularly the younger officers. Many of them were anti-American and in sympathy with fascist regimes, including the Argentinian Peronist variety. These officers were allied with a newly established Bolivian right-wing party named Movimiento Nacionalista Revolucionario (MNR), led by an ambitious young lawyer named Victor Paz Estenssoro. I had met Estenssoro two years earlier when he was in private law practice and was an office neighbor of mine. At the time, he had expressed very strong pro-Nazi leanings. He would later become President of Bolivia and an advocate of an extreme left-wing philosophy. The validity of the French saying, "*les extremes se touchent*," was confirmed by this political scenario.

I reported my findings to my boss at the American embassy, who said that he would report them to Washington.

Apparently, however, the State Department preferred to believe the ambassador's report and did not want to "rock the boat." The State Department was rudely expelled from its fool's paradise when, a year and a half later, a revolution broke out in Bolivia, toppling Peñaranda and installing a military *junta* of right-wing officers led by Villaroel in alliance with Victor Paz Estenssoro.

One morning in late 1944, word spread throughout La Paz that a revolution was in progress. A group of military officers headed by General Villaroel had formed an alliance with the MNR of Victor Paz Estenssoro, which had removed Peñaranda and formed a new revolutionary government. When the followers of the new government organized demonstrations throughout La Paz, shouting wild anti-American slogans, two Marines were posted in front of the U.S. embassy building to protect it against any eventuality. Most of the embassy personnel, including me, watched the goings-on in the streets from the rooftop. Since the president's private residence was in the immediate vicinity of the embassy building, we could see looters carrying away contents of the residence, including the plumbing, which was a most valuable commodity in Bolivia.

The new regime did not lose much time in persecuting and terrorizing its political adversaries and encouraging anti-Semitic incidents. A number of the junta's opponents, among them the distinguished editor of *La Razón*, an outstanding daily paper, disappeared (Argentinian style) and never returned. Vicious anti-American and anti-Jewish propaganda was unleashed through the press, radio, and in leaflets. This sent shock waves through the ranks of the Jewish refugees who had hoped to find a haven in Bolivia. The Jewish community sought intervention by the United States embassy, and I became the Jews' unofficial representative. As a result of my intervention with the ambassador, the ministers of the Villaroel regime were put on notice that unless they immediately put an end to anti-American and anti-Semitic actions, American aid and supplies would be placed in jeopardy. The junta understood this blunt language and acted accordingly.

Through my work at the American embassy I became acquainted with a number of interesting people. One day Ursula and I were invited by the American ambassador to a garden party to meet the visiting vice-president of the United States, Henry A. Wallace. Wallace was touring South America on behalf of President Roosevelt to convey the message that the United States was firmly committed to the so-called "Good Neighbor Policy" and intended to maintain close and friendly relations with the Latin American countries.

During my conversation with Wallace, he explained that it was the firm intention of the Roosevelt Administration to encourage democratic development in Latin America after the war. He added that this could be accomplished only by improvement of the lot of the "common man" through massive aid to education and economic reform. Interestingly enough, these efforts were taken up about twenty years later by President Kennedy's "Alliance for Progress" program.

Wallace also seemed to be acquainted with Jewish life in the United States, and asked me whether I was a Reform or Orthodox Jew. He was a most interesting person, and seemed familiar with the socio-economic problems of the Pacific Coast countries of South America. However, Roosevelt dumped him as his running mate for his fourth term and replaced him with Senator Harry Truman.

Above: City Hall (Rathaus), built in the fifteenth century.

Below: Neue Synagoge built in 1872, gutted by the Nazis during Kristallnacht, November 9, 1938.

My sister Lilli at age 12, and I at age 10.

Myself shortly before emigration, late 1938.

*My mother
(1938)*

*My father
(circa 1937)*

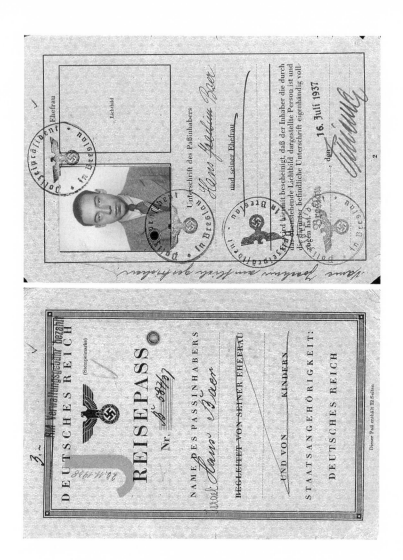

*Inside pages of my passport, issued in 1935,
with my middle name effaced.*

The photographs were taken last night as the refugees from the Chilean steamer Imperial, which docked here, were given shore leave.

Exiled Jews Head For Movies As First Refugee Boat Arrives

143 Stop Here On Way To Begin New Lives In South American Countries

(Continued from Page 2)

English is misinterpreted, our relatives might be held to blame if our names were known."

They posed readily for pictures, but refused to tell photographers what names to use for captions.

Visitors were struck by the apparent carefree, happy attitudes of these exiles.

"We are happy we are no longer in Germany," they said. "We hope for the future."

again that the Jews still in Germany must have help.

"Successful Jews in all parts of the world must raise funds to help these unfortunates out of a country where they are not wanted," they said.

Want To Help Relatives

"We want to succeed in our new lives so that we may send funds back to rescue our relatives.

"You would hardly believe how much the Jews in Germany are count-

*Front page of the Baltimore Sun,
January 11, 1939.*

ADLAI E. STEVENSON
231 So. LaSalle Street
Chicago

My dear friend –

Ever so many thanks for your message. It warmed my heart!

If I troubled the nation's sleep a little I am satisfied. Yet I regret that I could not better fulfill the hopes and expectations of my friends.

For your kindness and confidence I shall be forever grateful.

Faithfully yours,

Adlai S. Stevenson

Adlai Stevenson's letter to me after his unsuccessful presidential campaign against Eisenhower in 1952.

Marta Feuchtwanger,
flanked by Ursula and me,
circa 1978.

Ursula and I at Malibu beach, circa 1946.

Ursula and I at an Austrian "Heurigen" party, circa 1985.

*Top row, left to right: my granddaugher Michal's husband,
my grandson Dan, my granddaugher Tamar,
my son-in-law Victor (my daughter Leslie's husband).
Bottom row, left to right: my granddaughter Michal with her daugher
Ariella Yael, my son-in-law Elie, his wife (my daughter Gabriela),
my youngest daughter Leslie with my granddaughter Julia.*

*Birgitta and I,
1993.*

*My sister Lilli
(left), with Leslie
and me, circa
1991.*

*Giving a ride to my
youngest grand-
daughter, Julia,
1996.*

AMERICA

AT THE END OF 1944, when the victory of the Allies over Germany and Japan was within reach, I was called into the ambassador's office. The ambassador told me that I had rendered outstanding service to the United States, even though I was not an American citizen, and asked if there was anything that he could do for me, since he expected to be called home soon. I replied that I would be very happy if he could help me and my family immigrate to the United States. He said that he would gladly be of assistance and that he would arrange for a personal appearance before the immigration board in Washington when he returned to the States.

During the war, immigration to the U.S. had come to an almost complete standstill and only special cases were being considered before an immigration panel including representatives of the armed forces and the FBI.

A month or so later the ambassador returned to Bolivia and told me that he had in fact appeared before the immigration board and in the course of questioning had been asked why I wanted to come to the United States. His answer had been "for the same reason that your forefathers and mine came to these shores, for the privilege of becoming an American citizen." He told me he expected to hear of the board's decision soon. A few weeks later the Consul General, a good friend of mine, called me into his office and asked me, "When do you want to leave for the United States?" He said that there was only one "technical" problem, namely that I had been married "by proxy" and that this type of marriage was not recognized in the United States. He called in the legal advisor to the embassy for a solution to this problem. The legal advisor stated a principle of American law with which I would become familiar a few years later during my study of "conflicts of laws." A marriage which is valid where contracted is valid everywhere. That did it for the Consul General, who issued visas for my entire family after two of my friends, Sproesser Wynn, the Fort Worth lawyer, and H.C. Cobbe, our bussiness manager, had signed the requisite Affidavits of Support as my sponsors. Since I was stateless, having been expatriated by the Nazi regime, Bolivia issued a stateless travel paper bearing the visas for myself and my family. My in-laws received a similar document, as they were included as visa beneficiaries.

We all were as if in a trance. Our dream to emigrate to the United States, the land of freedom and opportunities, had become a reality.

Still, we were not quite sure of our destination in the United States. One of our sponsors, my immediate superior officer at the embassy and a good friend, Sproessor Wynn, was a great patriot of the "Republic of Texas" and encouraged us to settle there, preferably in Fort Worth. He claimed that Fort Worth was an ideal community for bringing up children, as it was far from the sound and fury of the big cities of the United States. On the other hand, several of my co-workers at the embassy who were from California extolled the beautiful climatic advantages and economic future of Southern California. After weighing their arguments we tentatively decided to go to Fort Worth.

Traveling from South America to the United States during the war was no easy undertaking, since air travel was almost entirely monopolized by U.S. and South American government officials, resulting in a long waiting list of private travelers. Accordingly, we decided to travel from La Paz to the port city of Arica, Chile, by train and from there by boat to

Guayaquil, Ecuador, where we would take one of the banana boats bound for New Orleans.

Our day of departure was set for April 26, 1945, my birthday, shortly before V-E Day. The platform at the railroad station in La Paz was crowded with friends bidding us farewell.

The next morning we arrived at Arica, Chile, to meet the S.S. *Teno*, which was to take us to Guayaquil. The *Teno* was a rather small boat. It carried cattle on the lower deck and passengers on the upper deck. The odor wafting to our quarters from the lower deck was not exactly comparable to Chanel No. 5. Gaby, who at that time was just over three years old, became terribly seasick. The ship's doctor insisted that she had a "rare disease" and should be seen by a doctor immediately after the ship docked at Callao, Peru. The so-called "rare disease" disappeared immediately as soon as we stepped on terra firma.

In Callao, we were met by friends who had come down from Lima. We stayed in Lima for two or three days before continuing our voyage north along the west coast of South America. A few days later we sailed up the Guayas River to Guayaquil, Ecuador.

Guayaquil is the second largest city in Ecuador, characterized at that time by its swamp-like climate and its oversized *cucarachas*, or cockroaches. There, to our great disappointment, we learned that all steamship traffic between Ecuador and the United States had been discontinued. Thus we were stranded, and the Panagra (Panamerican-Grace) airline office informed us that it would be several months before we could expect to obtain air transportation to the United States.

In order to avoid depleting our meager resources I started looking for a job, and found one as a Spanish-English correspondent with a local bank. Meanwhile we made every effort to expedite the continuation of our voyage to the United States. Finally, after about three weeks, thanks to my persuasive powers and a generous tip (South American style), I was successful: I was told that there would be space for us on a flight to Miami, Florida, in three days.

While we were very happy with this good news, another

problem arose. We had taken our little dog, Blackie, with us from Bolivia, but now we were told by the airline that no animals were permitted aboard the plane. We had the choice of either giving the dog away or having her put to sleep in Guayaquil. Since we knew practically nobody in Guayaquil to whom we could entrust Blackie, we were faced with a most unpalatable choice. However, my mother-in-law, a most determined and resourceful lady, came up with another solution. She made a handbag with holes in it out of a Dirndl dress, and she hid the little dog in this bag.

It seemed as though Blackie knew what was at stake, for the dog behaved in exemplary fashion during the trip to the United States. Fortunately, the trip proceeded in stages over several days. After a short flight from Guayaquil, we landed at Cali, Colombia, where we stayed overnight. The next day we proceeded to Medellín, and from there to Barranquilla. While we were walking down the main avenue in Barranquilla, we were stopped by the driver of a car who asked us whether we were from Breslau. It turned out that he had been one of our neighbors.

From Barranquilla we flew to Miami, with stops in Kingston, Jamaica, which at the time was a British colony, and Camaguey, Cuba. After the passport inspection in Kingston, two British intelligence agents approached my father-in-law, George Bohm, and asked him whether he had a brother in Brazil by the name of Herman Bohm. When my father-in-law said that he did, the agents started interrogating him about his past activities. I intervened and showed the agents our travel papers, which contained the American Ambassador's request "to whomever it may concern" for the protection of my family. That did it. My father-in-law was released, and the agents apologized by saying that they were looking for a German agent named Herman Bohm, allegedly residing in Rio de Janeiro, who also had a brother named George.

In Miami, we were met by immigration officials and an agent of the FBI, as all immigrants had to be screened by the FBI during the war. The FBI agent, who obviously had been tipped off about our arrival, shook hands with me and said

"Welcome, Mr. Baer, to the United States. I know you will be a very good citizen." I was delighted with this welcome, which seemed to augur well for our future in the United States.

In the course of the subsequent customs inspection, my mother-in-law had to open her cloth bag, and out jumped the little dog. The customs officials had a lot of fun with Blackie and shared their lunch with her while the representative of the airline had a fit.

After checking into a hotel in Miami we took a walk through the city center. Since the United States was a country at war, with priorities of food supplies for the military, we had expected to see long lines in front of grocery stores. We saw no such thing; although, as we found out later, certain items such as sugar and cigarettes were rationed, nobody suffered any deprivation.

Later in the day we decided to have dinner in one of the cafeterias. We could not believe our eyes: we saw busboys carrying away enormous amounts of food which the patrons had left on their plates. Having just arrived from La Paz, where every morning the Indios and the dogs scrambled for the scant leftovers of spoiled food in the city dumps, we were utterly stunned. We were also shocked at the sight of "For Coloreds" signs displayed on water fountains, in restaurants, and other public places.

While in Miami I met one of my former supervisors at the U.S. embassy in La Paz, who had since become export manager of National Silver's office in Miami. He offered me a job as his assistant. I declined, as the hot and humid climate of Miami in June did not attract us. I made a telephone call to one of our sponsors, Sproesser Wynn, who now was a partner of a large law firm in Fort Worth, Texas. He told me to come to Fort Worth, where he would help us get settled. We took the train to Fort Worth via Chattanooga, Texarkana, and Memphis. The trip took two and one half days, as the train made numerous stops to take on servicemen headed for the West Coast, whence they expected to be shipped to the Pacific theater. The war against Germany had ended in early May, and now the United States was concentrating all of its efforts to defeat Japan.

Fort Worth was a pleasant medium-sized town. But after a few days my hope of obtaining a job with an import-export firm faded. Sproesser Wynn told me that one of his clients was interested in meeting me and in offering me employment. It turned out that his friend was the owner of an exterminating company that needed inspectors. Since termites are large and numerous in Texas, this looked like a profitable venture, though not exactly my line of work.

Following Horace Greeley's admonition "Go west, young man," my family and I took the next train to the Golden State, bound for Los Angeles. After a three-day trip through West Texas, New Mexico, Arizona, and the California desert, we arrived at Union Station on a cloudy day in June 1945. From the railroad station we telephoned Ursula's cousin, Margot Bland, who at the time lived off Venice Boulevard near La Cienega Boulevard. She told us to take a taxi and come to her house immediately. The taxi driver took full advantage of our status as greenhorns. Unbeknownst to us, he gave us the grand tour of the sprawling city of Los Angeles before he took us to our destination for a cab fare of almost $10.00, which, at the time, was a lot of money. Cousin Margot and her husband, Herbert, received us most cordially.

I was struck by the immensity of this city, which consisted and still consists of a large number of communities and thousands of neighborhoods. At that time, Los Angeles had no skyscrapers; most people had their own little houses with well-kept front lawns and backyards. The tallest building in Los Angeles at the time was City Hall. Los Angeles seemed to be the most unplanned city I had ever seen. The public transportation system consisted of trolley cars and the so-called Red Car system, which connected the downtown area with the beach communities, the San Fernando Valley (which then consisted of chicken farms), Pasadena, and other outlying communities. Almost everyone had a car.

All residential construction had come to a stop at the outbreak of the war, and there was an acute shortage of rental property, which was subject to strict rent control. Thus we had difficulty finding permanent lodging. The first few months we stayed in a boarding house on West 6th Street overlooking MacArthur Park, which at the time was still a respectable neighborhood. A few months later we moved into a rebuilt garage on South Harvard Avenue between Adams and Jefferson.

This was not exactly a choice neighborhood. All five of us, plus our dog, were crammed into this garage, which as far as I remember consisted of a tiny kitchen with a breakfast nook, a living room with a couch that could be converted into a bed for my in-laws, and an adjacent small bedroom for Ursula, myself, and Gaby. That "luxurious" flat was endowed with a fascinating type of shower. When the shower was turned on and the water rushed down, the ants which had settled in the shower area moved in the opposite direction.

After a year and a half we rented a cottage on the corner of McCadden and Selma in Hollywood, a much better residential area.

Within a few days after our arrival we started looking for jobs. My mother-in-law got the first job. She went to work as a "practical nurse" for an old, heavy invalid whom she, a woman weighing only 100 pounds, had to lift from his bed twice a day. My father-in-law landed a job as a shipping clerk (and later as shipping manager) with a ceramics distributor on North Hoover near Temple Street, where he had to prepare and lift heavy packages for shipment. Ursula found work taking care of a little boy in the Boyle Heights district while his parents were working.

I figured that my linguistic abilities might be put to good use by the international department of a local bank. Therefore, I went from bank to bank until, after about a week, I was hired by the manager of the foreign department of Union Bank, a Swiss by the name of Leo C. Helfenberger. We remained friends until his death in 1992.

Our respective salaries, which we pooled, were anything but lavish. Still, we were happy to get started in the new country. My base salary was $150 per month. Even at that time, when the dollar bought much more than today, it was a most meager income. Therefore I tried to increase my income by working overtime. In addition, during the Christmas season I went to work for Bullocks department store, which was one block away, as shipping clerk from 6:00 P.M. to 9:00 P.M. It was soon discovered that making packages was not exactly my forte. One day the manager of the shipping department approached me with the suggestion that I go to work in a different department where my talent in areas other than shipping could be put to more efficient use.

Another source of additional income was to open up a few months after our arrival. One day I met an elderly bearded gentleman who came to the bank for advice on a money transfer to Europe. He spoke with a European accent, and within a few minutes we discovered that we had a lot in common. It turned out that he was Rabbi Jacob Sonderling, originally from Hamburg, who had studied at the Theological Seminary in Breslau around the turn of the century. He was the rabbi of the Fairfax Temple, which served mostly immigrants from Germany, Austria, and Czechoslovakia. He asked me to take over the secretarial duties at his temple, working at the temple office two to three evenings a week for $50 a month. In addition, I was to teach Sunday school there. Since we did not have a car in a city where a car was a virtual necessity, this meant that I would have to take the bus between our home in the Western-Adams district, and Fairfax Avenue three evenings a week. My duties consisted of keeping the membership records of the temple up to date and taking care of incoming and outgoing correspondence. However, when the good rabbi asked me after a few months to take over the collection of dues from delinquent members and to help the temple raise funds, I told him that he needed a full-time secretary at full-time pay. Nevertheless, I stayed on as Sunday school teacher for almost two years.

While my job in the foreign department of Union Bank did not pay enough to eke out even a frugal living, it gave me insights into international finance in the fields of import and export. Every day after three o'clock, when the doors of the bank closed, I had to balance our books to reflect the receipts and disbursements of the day, and woe to me if I was off by even as little as five cents.

After the books had been balanced, I and my colleague, an immigrant from Vienna, disappeared for about twenty minutes to have coffee and pastries around the corner on Broadway in a very popular restaurant named Pig 'n Whistle. I enjoyed looking at a fresco on the wall of the restaurant. It portrayed two fellows, one of whom was looking at a donut while the other one exclaimed, "As you go through life, brother, whatever be your goal, keep your eye upon the donut and not upon the hole." This philosophy expresses my own thinking and approach to life; if you permit yourself to be overwhelmed by problems and disappointments, you will remain a prisoner of your own fears. However, if you decide to count your blessings and consider your problems as challenges, you will fill your life with meaning and a sense of fulfillment.

After working for the bank for about a year and a half, I decided to move on and took a job as assistant manager with a newly established manufacturer of plastic toys on Higuera Street in Culver City opposite the backlot of the Metro-Goldwyn-Mayer studio. After a few months it turned out that the line of toys did not enjoy much popularity, and since the owner was not prepared to change, he closed his business, leaving me without a job.

Fortunately, my unemployment did not last long. I remembered a company by the name of Southwest Steel Rolling Mills, whose account I had handled while working for Union Bank. This company was owned by Lester and Ruben Finkelstein, who operated a steel mill in the South Gate area on Alameda Street. I called on their personnel manager and was employed as assistant export manager. He told me, "We will pay you a decent salary, but you will never get as much as you think you are worth." He certainly kept his word.

My bosses were the sons of Russian-Jewish immigrants who

had come to Los Angeles around 1890 from Odessa and set up the first scrap-metal operation in Los Angeles. In the late 1930s the two brothers started operating a steel mill, the first on the West Coast. Both brothers were self-made men. Lester was the more dynamic and imaginative of the two. His outstanding abilities in marketing were paired with his abysmal failure in personal relations with the people who worked for him, for most of whom he had little regard. Over his desk there was a picture portraying an executive screaming at his trembling employee "Don't 'yes' me. Tell me what you think even if it costs you your job!"

For this reason, few of the company's employees stayed longer than two or three years. I, on the other hand, worked for him a total of fifteen years, even though I had to fight Lester every time I felt I was due for a raise. He seemed to respect my initiative and ability to establish and maintain foreign markets for his products. The field of construction steel products (reinforcing steel and girders) was completely new to me. However, in a few weeks I had read enough about steel products to enable me to sell them in foreign markets. During the immediate postwar period, following the complete destruction of the European and Japanese steel industries, the United States was practically the only source of steel in the world. Therefore, the steel export market offered excellent opportunities. After a few years I became export manager and took several extended trips throughout Latin America and to Japan, a country which fascinated me and of which I have many fond memories. They include the trip that Ursula and I took in 1958 when, unbeknownst to either of us, she was pregnant with our younger daughter, Leslie.

In order to supplement my income, I soon started looking for additional part-time employment. Since I was a linguist with command of six languages and very fond of teaching, I was interested in conducting adult evening courses in Spanish, French, or German. After obtaining my teaching credentials from Sacramento, I was hired by the principal of Inglewood High School, which needed an instructor in Spanish for its adult courses.

This was the McCarthy era, and everybody who was politically left of dead center was suspected of being a Communist or a "fellow-traveler." It was the time when authors and screenwriters of Hollywood films who had expressed "liberal" ideas were hauled before the House Un-American Activities Committee. They were rendered unemployable or even jailed unless they "recanted," giving up their First Amendment rights, and told "the truth" about their thoughts, their activities, and those of their friends and associates suspected of "Communist" or "liberal" ideas.

This was the darkest time of attempted thought control and political intimidation that I ever experienced in the "Land of the Free." Its architects were Senator McCarthy, Richard Nixon, Senator Knowland from California, and Senator Karl Mundt from South Dakota. Contrary to the constitutional presumption of innocence until proven guilty, every person who sought public employment had to take the so-called "loyalty oath." This involved the disclosure of an applicant's political affiliation, past and present, showing that he or she was entitled to a political clean bill of health. Consequently, before being employed by the evening school system, I had to sign this odious declaration.

My Spanish courses were scheduled for two evenings a week from six o'clock to nine o'clock. It turned out to be a most enjoyable experience, and I met many interesting people. During the first session of my class I asked each student the reason for his or her attendance. The answer I received from one lady, who turned out to be a very good student, was "because I always wanted to visit Rio de Janeiro." When I told her that she was in the wrong pew, she answered, "This doesn't matter; I will postpone my trip to Rio."

Since there was very little useful material available for these courses, I made up my own syllabus, which proved highly successful. I taught these courses for two or three years, until my overseas trips prevented me from continuing.

I still fondly remember the beautiful Christmas gift the class gave me when they took me to a well-known restaurant on Olvera Street named La Golondrina. It was a red tie with the embroidered words "El Profesor." I still have that tie and will always cherish the friendship which motivated the gift.

Another memorable experience of those early days was my introduction to the famous German-Jewish writer, Lion Feuchtwanger and his wife, Marta. They had fled from Germany to France in the early 1930s. When the Germans invaded France in May 1940, the Vichy regime put them in the infamous internment camp of Gurs, near Marseille, together with thousands of other refugees. Thanks to Marta's ingenuity they escaped, crossed the Pyrenees on foot, and went to Portugal, where, due to Eleanor Roosevelt's intervention, the American consul issued immigration visas to them, enabling them to come to the United States. They settled in Pacific Palisades in a beautiful house named Villa Aurora, with a breathtaking view of the Pacific. Villa Aurora soon became a center for other exiled German writers such as Thomas Mann, Heinrich Mann, and Berthold Brecht, to name but a few. Today it is an international meeting place of writers in residence and is becoming a cultural center in Southern California.

Lion Feuchtwanger was the author of a number of historical novels, among them *The Jewish War*, the story of Flavius Josephus, and a book entitled *Arms for America*, which soon became popular in the United States. In Pacific Palisades he continued writing novels, surrounded by one of the largest collections of books in several languages that I had ever seen, including first editions of well-known literary works and periodicals. I vividly remember spending a weekend at Villa Aurora a few years later, reading *Le Moniteur Universel*, the French official gazette, published during the French Revolution, containing the minutes of the trials of Louis XVI, referred to as *citoyen Louis Capet,* and of his nemesis, Robespierre.

A few times a year the Feuchtwangers would gather a circle of well-known exiled German authors, actors, composers, and scholars, together with a select group of professionals engaged in other fields of endeavor. At these gatherings, which soon became known as "Weimar II," Feuchtwanger would read from the novels on which he was currently working. There followed animated discussions ranging from literary to social and political subjects. The delicacies which Marta Feuchtwanger would serve the guests made a welcome contribution to the attraction of these evenings.

At these literary evenings, I had the pleasure and privilege of meeting some of the outstanding representatives of German literature in exile: Thomas Mann, his brother Heinrich Mann, Berthold Brecht, author of the *Three Penny Opera*, Ludwig Marcuse, and Harold von Hofe, distinguished professor of German studies and subsequently Dean of the German department at the University of Southern California. I sometimes participated in the discussions following Feuchtwanger's readings. One such discussion dealt with a chapter in his novel *Narrenweisheit* (*Fool's Wisdom*), a biography of Jean-Jacques Rousseau. In this chapter a representative of the newly formed United States of America exalts the lofty principles of liberty and equality proclaimed by the former American colonies in a dialogue with a prominent French citizen. I pointed to the gulf which still separated ideal and reality in American life 175 years after the proclamation of these principles.

After Lion Feuchtwanger's death, I became Marta Feuchtwanger's legal adviser. She was a frequent and most welcome dinner guest at our home. Whenever she visited us she gave us one of Lion's books with a gracious dedication. She was the author of the last book which she gave us, entitled *Only a Woman*, a remarkable autobiography.

Most of the writers, artists, and scholars who gathered at Villa Aurora in the 1940s considered themselves exiles. While I also met the technical definition of an exile, I did not feel that I was going into exile at the time of my emigration from Germany or at any time thereafter. I did feel like an exile in 1933 when the Nazis came to power and made me a pariah in the land of my birth. However, when I emigrated five years later I was overcome by a feeling of relief and liberation from oppression, determined to build a new life in the New World and not to return to Germany. This feeling, which was no doubt shared by most other Jewish refugees, contrasted with those of most non-Jewish German refugees from the Nazi regime. They had left Germany for political reasons and intended to return to their homeland after Hitler's fall.

Another group which I joined shortly after taking up residence in Los Angeles was the Jewish Club of 1933. This group was founded in 1934 by Jewish refugees from Germany, Austria, and Czechoslovakia for the purpose of mutual assistance, or "networking" as we would say today. The club not only aided its members materially by helping them find employment and to become integrated into their new country, but also lifted their spirits by offering them cultural programs such as concerts, recitals, lectures, and other social events. It included a number of outstanding persons who had occupied leading positions in the public life of their native lands. One of these persons, who became a leader of the Jewish Club in those early days, was Leopold Jessner, former director of the Staatstheater (State Theater) in Berlin. Another outstanding member was the well-known architect Richard Neutra. However, the most challenging problem confronting the club and its members was yet to come.

Shortly after Pearl Harbor, the U.S. Military Command on the West Coast headquartered in San Francisco called for the removal and relocation of all "enemy aliens" from the West Coast. This order included Nazi Germans as well as German Jewish refugees who had not as yet acquired U.S. citizenship. Their internment in special "relocation camps," like the internment of the Japanese-Americans, was a distinct possibility. The Jewish Club rose to the challenge. Its leaders immediately asked Congress to intervene and stop the order. A Senate committee known as the Tolan Committee went to California to hold hearings. Its members included the then Senator Harry S. Truman. Thomas Mann, an honorary member of the Club, and Bruno Frank, both outstanding German writers, assisted by Professor Jessner, pointed out to the committee the differences between German immigrants and the "Hitler immigrants."

Simultaneously, a telegram urging the rescision of the

evacuation order was sent to President Franklin D. Roosevelt signed by Arturo Toscanini, Count Carlos Sforza, Albert Einstein, Bruno Walter, and Thomas Mann.

As a result of these efforts, the evacuation order was withdrawn.

Nevertheless, for the duration of the war, German-Jewish refugees who had not yet acquired U.S. citizenship were included in the 8:00 P.M. curfew and subjected to travel restrictions except by special permission.

In later years, after the former refugees had integrated themselves into the economic life of their new homeland, the Jewish Club continued its beneficent work on the cultural, social, and charitable levels. It is still an active organization, and while many, if not most, of their early members are no longer with us, there is still a core of dedicated people of the first and second generations. Moreover, over the years the Jewish Club has become one of the main support groups for the Jewish Home for the Aging in the San Fernando Valley.

C · h · a · p · t · e · r S · i · x

LEGAL CAREER

WHILE MY WORK DURING the daytime and in the evening was interesting and enabled me to make a decent living, I decided after a few years to prepare for building a professional career and to become a lawyer.

What created my interest in the study and practice of law?

As a student of Talmudic law at the Breslau Theological Seminary, I was fascinated by the spirited debates of the rabbis over the interpretation of the laws of the Bible and their application to the problems of everyday life. Several years later, two men whom I had met in the course of my employment at the American embassy in Bolivia encouraged me to take up the study of law after my arrival in the United States. These men were two eminent Texas lawyers, Philip Kazan, a former Texas state prosecutor, and Sproesser Wynn, an attorney with a prominent firm in Fort Worth. They introduced me to the principles of common law as the foundation of American law.

One day Sproesser Wynn said he felt that Bolivia could benefit from updating its laws on negotiable instruments, the law of bills and notes. He then challenged me, as a linguist, to translate the major portions of the U.S. Negotiable Instruments Act into Spanish. I rose to the challenge, and within several months the translation was ready. My friend Sproesser then had it introduced into the Bolivian legislature.

The project was extremely complicated, as it involved translation of many legal concepts into another language in which those concepts did not exist. The steady assistance I received from Sproesser in clarifying these concepts was indispensable for the completion of this project.

After taking up residence in Los Angeles I had to make a living, and my responsibilities as export manager of the steel company involved a daily schedule of ten to twelve hours. Therefore my enrollment in a law school requiring attendance at regular classes was out of the question. Thus, the only realistic possibility for me was to participate in a correspondence course. This type of course was offered by La Salle Extension University of Chicago, Illinois. Accordingly, I enrolled in this course and started the long-term preparation for a career as a lawyer.

I pored over law books almost every day after dinner and during weekends. Whenever I went on a trip I had my law books with me. Maintaining this grueling schedule for many years would have been impossible without the unflagging support and encouragement of my beloved Ursula, who took over all of the household responsibilities and never complained about the very limited amount of time that we could spend together.

However, there was one evening every week on which we allowed no intrusion. That was Saturday, when we would go to the movies either by ourselves or with our friends Sig and Anneliese Nathan.

Completion of my law studies took much longer than we had anticipated, mainly because from time to time I had to interrupt my studies temporarily under the pressures of my daytime responsibilities. I missed the stimulating give-and-take of regular classroom atmosphere, with its thought-provoking discussions and challenges under the direction of a good instructor. There were times when I felt discouraged and considered giving up my studies altogether. However, I would not give in to this mood for very long. The challenge of building my own future as a lawyer made me go on.

Another problem interfering with my studies was the need

for frequent business trips to Latin America, and later on in the late 1950s, to Japan in an effort to establish and expand markets for our products. Still, I never traveled without my law books.

I found Japan to be a fascinating country with hard-working people and almost no illiteracy. I remember that during my first visit to Tokyo, as I was walking the streets at night I noticed several brightly illuminated stores. I found out that these were bookstores packed with people who were reading or browsing.

Another interesting experience was my visit to a late-afternoon concert at Hibyia Park in the center of Tokyo. The orchestra played compositions by Dvorak, Schumann, and Mozart for a cross section of people of all ages. One could have heard a pin drop during the performance.

After my return to Los Angeles from that first trip to Japan, I took up the study of the Japanese language for about eight or ten months in order to be able to carry on at least a light conversation during my next trip. When I arrived in Japan for my second visit, I was met at the airport by my late friend, Mr. Aiji Takahashi. I tried to engage him in a Japanese conversation, but he remained impassive. Finally I asked him what he thought of my Japanese. He asked me, "Do you want an American answer or a Japanese answer?" I replied, "An American answer." He answered, "I understand what you are trying to say, but you speak like a peasant." I countered that if I spoke like a Japanese peasant, I must have made some progress.

Shortly before leaving on my first trip to Japan, in 1956, I presented myself for the California bar exam. I failed and found out later that this was not due to ignorance of the law but to my lack of training in the presentation of the issues involved. Accordingly, I decided to take a bar review course. After its completion in spring 1957, I took the bar exam again, and this time I passed. The percentage of successful candidates at the time was approximately 28 percent. Since the country was in the throes of an economic recession at the time, I decided that it was not a propitious moment to leave my position as export manager and venture into the practice of law.

My daughter Gaby, who had been an excellent student, graduated from Hollywood High School in 1958 and became a college student at UCLA. Shortly thereafter, she met Elie Litov, an Israeli who had come to the United States a few years before. I believe it was in early 1959 that the two announced that they wanted to get married. Although Ursula and I liked Elie, we thought that it was too early for Gaby to get married; she was eighteen, which, by the way, was Ursula's age when she married me. Nevertheless, the two got married on January 30, 1960, and soon thereafter moved to Riverside, where both attended UC Riverside, Elie as a budding physicist and Gaby as a candidate for the degree of Master of Social Work. They presented us with our first grandchild, Dan, in 1961.

Another blessed event occurred in the late 1950s. In the fall of 1958, Ursula and I traveled to Japan as guests of our good friend, Aiji Takahashi, who resided in Kamakura, near Yokohama. During our trip, Ursula developed certain symptoms which made us suspect that there might soon be an addition to our family. When, upon our return to Los Angeles, our doctor announced to us that we would become parents again, I turned as white as a sheet, whereupon Dr. Lewin told Ursula, "Please drive him home. We have not lost a father yet." Eight months later, on May 22, 1959, our Leslie was born, a lovely child, easy to raise and love.

Several years later, in the fall of 1962, I decided to quit my position and hang out my shingle as a lawyer. This was quite a risk, as our financial resources were rather meager. Accordingly, we took a bank loan secured by a mortgage on our residence to permit us to make both ends meet until the first dollars from my practice started rolling in. I sub-rented a small office from the law firm of Shacknove and Goldman at Wilshire Boulevard and La Jolla, and was my own typist and secretary during the first year. During these first months of my practice I felt like a parachutist who had bailed out of an airplane with the prayer that the parachute would open up in time.

My first case was a petition in bankruptcy on behalf of a young couple who had opened up a coffeeshop on Ventura Boulevard and failed. I remember typing reams and reams of schedules on the Underwood typewriter, working days, nights, and weekends.

My second case was a personal injury matter against the City of Los Angeles, involving a lady who had broken her leg as the result of the defective condition of the sidewalk in the Alvarado-Third Street area of Los Angeles. My investigation disclosed that the defective condition had existed for a considerable length of time. I was thus able to prove that the city had had "constructive notice" of the defect. I succeeded in settling this matter, and earned the fabulous fee of $500. We decided to spend part of it on a weekend trip to beautiful Coronado, across the bay from San Diego.

More cases followed. Since I had no trial experience, I decided to associate with the law firm of Shacknove and Goldman in cases involving litigation. I still remember a divorce case in which I represented the wife. The husband, owner of a trucking company, had been ordered by the court to submit the books and records of his firm. When he arrived in court, he claimed his offices had been burglarized the night before and that most of his records, had been taken by the burglars. I remember Judge Pfaff directing him to catch the burglars within twenty-four hours or go to jail. The "burglars" were soon caught, and the books and records retrieved and presented to the court. They disclosed that the firm was doing very well. As a result, the husband was ordered to pay a substantial alimony to his wife.

In July 1963 my associates and I moved to a newly established development called Century City on land formerly owned by Twentieth Century Fox studios. We thought this project had great potential as a business and professional center for the western part of Los Angeles. Our expectations turned out to be justified.

At the early stage of my practice, I took all sorts of cases, including criminal and divorce cases. I remember representing a husband who sought a divorce from his wife on the grounds of incompatibility. There were two small children. Since it appeared to me that an attempt should be made to reconcile the spouses, I had both of them in my office on a Saturday afternoon. As a result they reconciled. However, when I sent my client the bill he refused to pay on the grounds that I had been hired to file a divorce action. He added that since this purpose had not been achieved, I was not entitled to a fee.

An interesting criminal case was one involving a young man, a German who had put ads in the paper claiming that he was in a position to put together extremely cheap charter flights to Europe provided he got a $25 "registration fee." Many people had fallen for this scam, and one disgruntled person who had spent $25 had reported him to the mail fraud section of the U.S. Postal Service. He had subsequently been convicted of mail fraud and placed in the county jail in downtown Los Angeles.

The German consulate, whose legal advisor I had become in the meantime, contacted me and asked whether I could give him legal assistance. I visited the young man in the downtown jail. He claimed that he was wasting his time in jail, since he had so many more plans. I told him that I felt that the only way for him to get out of jail quickly was for me to convince our federal authorities that since he was a foreigner it would be a waste of the taxpayers' money to keep him in jail, and that the U.S. was better served by having him deported.

While these negotiations were going on, the young man was transferred to the Terminal Island federal prison, where I tried to visit him. Upon my arrival at Terminal Island I was advised that he had escaped by mingling with the Sunday afternoon visitors, and was being sought by federal authorities. However, the young man made one mistake. Right after his escape he contacted his former girlfriend. Unbeknownst to him, his girlfriend had in the meantime found solace in the arms of another man. While my client was at his ex-girlfriend's apartment, she made a call to the FBI, who promptly appeared on the scene to escort the young man back to federal prison.

Another fascinating case involved an elderly French couple residing in Paris. Their daughter and her husband had a child, a girl of about six or seven years, whom I shall call "Denise." After the mother's death the grandparents asked the French *Cour des Tutelles* (guardianship court) for custody of Denise. The court granted the grandparents custody rights and weekend visitation rights to the father.

One weekend, however, the father did not return his daughter to her grandparents. It was subsequently discovered that the girl's father had purchased an airline ticket to California with a "rubber" check, and that both he and the little girl had left Paris for Los Angeles, where the young man had two sisters.

One day the grandparents appeared in my office requesting that I take the necessary steps to help them ascertain the whereabouts of their granddaughter and take custody of her.

This obviously involved not only legal services, but also detective work. We hired a detective, who contacted the young man's two sisters in the Los Angeles area. As was to be expected, they denied any knowledge of their brother's whereabouts.

A few days later I had a "brainstorm." It appeared to me that this case should be presented as a human-interest story on TV stations, including the display of Denise's photograph. I pursued this idea and a few days later, one of the TV stations arranged for an interview of the grandparents and me in my office. In the course of the interview we exhibited recent snapshots of the little girl and of her father. We indicated that the father was being sought by the authorities and requested that members of the audience immediately call the TV station or the police in the event that any one of them should see someone resembling Denise or her father.

About a week later we received a call from the TV station. They had been contacted by a woman in the San Diego area who had noticed a man and a little girl who looked like Denise's father and Denise at the Greyhound depot, where they were getting on a bus for Lake Tahoe. We immediately notified our detective, who lost no time in flying to the Bay

Area. He soon contacted us with the information that he had located Denise's father, who was working as a cab driver. He also told us that Denise was attending grade school in the Lake Tahoe area. I informed Denise's grandparents, who were in Los Angeles at the time, and suggested that we take immediate legal action for her removal from her father's control and for restoration of custody to them. However, her grandparents decided on a different course of action.

A few days later the detective called me to report on developments that had taken place. He told me that Denise's grandparents had flown to the Bay Area and had been waiting in front of the school gate in the afternoon when classes were over. When Denise saw her grandparents she immediately rushed into their arms and clung to them. The detective took Denise and her grandparents into a waiting car and drove them to San Francisco, where they boarded a Paris-bound plane.

But, the story did not end there, as it probably would have if it had been a TV script rather than reality. When Denise's father found out what had happened he left for Paris, and— believe it or not —took her grandparents to court. In its decision, which, in my opinion, can only be called a miscarriage of justice, the French court ruled that, regardless of the illegal means Denise's father had used in getting her out of France, her grandparents should have taken her father to court in California rather than resorting to self-help. The court apparently disregarded the fact that we had obtained a writ of *habeas corpus* from the Los Angeles Superior Court. This writ directed any law enforcement officer in the State of California to obtain Denise's custody from her father and to bring her to court for proper disposition of the case. Obviously, the reason why this writ could not be enforced was Denise's unlawful concealment by her father. Accordingly, in giving her father custody rights while limiting the grandparents' rights to weekly visitation, the court virtually rewarded Denise's father for his outrageous conduct.

A few months later, when I visited Paris, I had a conference with Denise's grandparents and their French lawyer. Our meeting took place during a delicious lunch at the beautiful restaurant La Perigourdine on the left bank of the River Seine near Place St. Michel. I left Paris soon thereafter and learned later that Denise's grandparents and their son-in-law had reached a settlement with respect to Denise's custody.

During my latest visit to Paris, in summer 1996, Denise's grandparents, who had graciously invited me to a delicious luncheon after a visit to their apartment at Chateau Vincennes (Paris), introduced me to Denise, a lovely young lady in her twenties. She had insisted on taking a day off from her job at Disneyland near Paris in order to meet me. It was a memorable moment.

Fortunately, my law practice continued expanding, particularly in the field of international law, including international trade as well as private and public international law. In the field of international trade, my background in imports and exports stood me in good stead, and I was able to give legal guidance to American firms in their marketing problems with foreign agents, distributors, buyers, and joint ventures, as well as to foreign firms seeking a foothold in the California market. At the same time I became legal counsel to a constantly increasing number of consulates and trade commissioners stationed in Southern California. This responsibility required a thorough knowledge of international treaties and federal legislation on subjects such as arbitration, taxation, and immunities and privileges of foreign governments and their consular representatives in cases of legal disputes.

My professional activities provided me with the opportunity to meet several prominent persons. One of them was Maestro Carlo Maria Giulini, one of the former conductors of the Los Angeles Philharmonic Orchestra. He was introduced to me by one of my Italian friends, and asked that I represent him in negotiating his contract with Mr. Ernest Fleischmann, the executive director of the Los Angeles Philharmonic Association. Accordingly, I proceeded with the negotiation of the agreement between the maestro and the Los Angeles Philharmonic Association. Personal reasons compelled Maestro

Giulini to leave Los Angeles before the end of his term; his wife, Marcella, had fallen gravely ill and Maestro Giulini wanted to return to Italy.

Meeting Maestro Giulini and his wife was indeed a privilege. He was a very private person who lived for his music and did not wish to be encumbered by social engagements. When he raised the baton, he lived in a different world and was impervious to everything that went on around him. His favorite piece was Verdi's *Requiem*. His wife, Marcella, was a wonderful and practical woman. She took care of all the daily chores of the family so that her husband could devote himself entirely to his art. It was mostly she with whom I discussed the problems which I had in connection with the negotiations of the contract with the L.A. Philharmonic Orchestra and its implementation.

One day Marcella invited Ursula and me to a "very simple Italian dinner" at her beautiful home in the Hollywood Hills. The "simple dinner" Marcella had prepared turned out to be a most delicious and elaborate Italian meal, washed down by several bottles of chianti. During that memorable evening, Marcella and the Maestro told us about their families, their upbringing, and their experiences during World War II. Marcella told us how she and her parents had hidden a large number of Jews who would otherwise have been deported to the death camps by the Germans.

Another most interesting person whom I served as international lawyer was film director John Huston. I made his acquaintance in the mid-1980s. He was already gravely ill with emphysema and had to be transported by wheelchair. He always had an oxygen bottle with him, but despite his condition he was unable to stop smoking his cigars. He was a very modest and unassuming man, and told fascinating stories about his youth and his father, the famous Walter Huston. He died in the summer of 1987 while directing a movie in New England. At the time I was in France and learned of his death on French television.

My professional acquaintance with Ernst Krenek, a prominent Austrian opera composer who had to flee the Nazi regime, was a most pleasant experience. He and his wife, Gladys, lived in Palm Springs, where I visited them repeatedly. After his death several years ago, Gladys graciously gave me a copy of his fascinating biography.

Ironically, the first consulate that retained me as its lawyer was the consulate of the Federal Republic of Germany. As a former Jewish refugee from Nazi persecution whose family had been decimated by the Nazis, I had strong emotional reservations against the resumption of any kind of relationship with Germans. However, I found out that most of the members of the German consulate here belonged to the young generation which had grown up after the war. Most of them agreed with me that while they could not and should not be held responsible for the atrocities committed by or in the name of the previous generation, they carried a heavy responsibility for the future. The dialogues which I had with numerous members of the new generation were a most interesting and encouraging experience, which in many instances led to lasting personal friendships.

I wished that I could have witnessed another kind of dialogue—that between the members of the German postwar generation and their elders. What kind of answers did the latter give to their children when questioned about why they had caused or permitted a madman and his thugs to plunge Germany and the world into the worst catastrophe of the twentieth century, and to murder six million Jews and other minorities? Would their parents plead ignorance of these atrocities? Would they question that these events had ever happened? Or would they seek to gain their children's sympathy with recitals of their own sufferings during World War II?

My forthcoming relationships with consular and other representatives of Austria here in Southern California presented similar problems and challenges. I knew that Austria was a country in which anti-Semitism was as deeply rooted as in Germany, to say the least. When Hitler marched into Austria in March 1938, he certainly found an enthusiastic "victim." The fact that prominent Nazis, such as Eichmann,

Heydrich, and consorts, were Austrians, was no coincidence.

And yet Austria, in general, and Vienna in particular, had been among the main centers of Jewish creativity in Europe. Austria was home to people such as Arthur Schnitzler, Stefan Zweig, Max Reinhardt, Arnold Schoenberg, and Sigmund Freud, to name but a few. Vienna had been the center of the Zionist movement at the time of Theodor Herzl, its founder, who had his domicile there at the turn of the century as a foreign correspondent and feuilletionist of the Vienna *Neue Freie Presse.*

Sometime in the late 1960s—I believe it was in 1969—I met the first Austrian Consul General appointed to Southern California, Dr. Thomas Klestil, a young and dynamic representative of the postwar generation, presently the president of the Austrian Republic. He asked me if I would be prepared to become the Consul General's legal counsel. I accepted. Out of this professional relationship grew a personal friendship with Dr. Klestil and his wife, Edith, which has endured to the present. Thomas Klestil and I had many frank discussions about Austrian-Jewish relations and the need to build bridges between the postwar generations on both sides. Through Dr. Klestil and his successors here in Los Angeles I had the opportunity of meeting a large number of Austrian officials and private citizens, many of whom expressed their sincere desire to help build a new democratic Austria and to fight the resurgence of anti-Semitism.

In addition to Germany and Austria, I became legal advisor to the consulates of France, Belgium, the Netherlands, Denmark, Spain, Canada, Australia, New Zealand, Italy, Sweden, and Finland as well as to the trade commissioners of most of these countries. I thoroughly enjoyed, and still enjoy, my professional and personal contacts with the international communities. I received decorations from Germany, Austria, Italy, and France. In 1993, France made me *Officier de la Legion du Merite,* one of the highest civilian decorations. In early 1997 the German Federal Republic awarded me an equally distinguished decoration, the *Grosses Bundesverdienstkreuz.*

C · h · a · p · t · e · r   S · e · v · e · n

THE NEW GERMANY

IN 1961 I VISITED GERMANY FOR the first time since my emigration in 1938, in order see my school friend Bibi Mott in Bonn and to discuss my restitution claims with Dr. Robert Kempner, a well-known lawyer and assistant to the prosecution at the Nurenberg Trials in 1946. A feeling of anxiety overcame me when the airplane approached the airport at Wahn, near Cologne. During the subsequent short train ride from Cologne to Bonn, I was seated across from a middle-aged, well-nourished German couple. All of a sudden, I saw this man in an SS uniform with the swastika armband, and imagined that the train was eastbound....

Shadows of the past dominated my first encounter with postwar Germany. Walking through the streets of Bonn and Frankfurt brought back haunting memories of dreadful days and nights in November 1938, when I wandered through the streets of Berlin to escape the dragnet of the Gestapo. I gave a sigh of relief when the plane took off from Frankfurt, bound for Israel via Rome.

My visit to Israel was the highlight of my trip, which subsequently took me to Hong Kong, Japan, Hawaii, and back to Los Angeles. I was in a prayerful mood when the plane touched down at the Lod Airport in Israel. The dream of a Jewish homeland, which many had dismissed as a pure fantasy, had become a visible reality to me.

During my second visit to Bonn, in the 1970s, shortly after I had been awarded a German decoration, I was received in audience by President Heinemann. The irony of history came over me when I, a former German Jew who had had to flee Germany for my life in 1938, was picked up about thirty-five years later by an envoy of the president of postwar Germany in an official automobile of the president's office and taken to the presidential palace for a private audience with the German chief of state.

Mr. Heinemann thanked me for my professional services to the Consulate General in Los Angeles. He added that while he realized that my visit to Germany would awaken painful memories, he wanted to assure me that the Germany which I found was and hopefully would remain a different country, firmly rooted in democratic institutions.

And yet, when I engage in dialogue with Germans about the Holocaust and the conclusions to be drawn from it by Germany's present and future generations, I often receive mixed signals. One reaction, usually coming from members of the second and third generation, is characterized by abhorrence of the atrocities committed against the Jews and an understanding of the bitterness felt by a large number of Jews against everything German. This understanding is often combined with resentment felt by members of the younger German generations for being held equally responsible with the older generation for the atrocities of the Holocaust committed at a time when many of them had not yet been born. It seems to me that the principles of justice, which are the foundation of Judaism, require us to respect this position. However, while postwar German generations should not be saddled with guilt for the past, theirs is the challenge to exercise perpetual vigilence.

There are other Germans who manifest impatience with our insistence on perpetuating the memory of the Holocaust. Some of them feel that the Jews should find it in their hearts to "forgive what happened fifty years ago" and to draw a *Schlusstrich*. This demand is often accompanied by expressions of self-pity and attempts to compare the deaths of thousands of German civilians by Allied bombardments with the murder of six million defenseless Jews in the gas ovens of Auschwitz and Treblinka. These reactions, which reflect utter reluctance to understand and learn from the past, deeply worry me and remind me of words spoken by the poet Heinrich Heine 150 years ago: *"Denk' ich an Deutschland in der Nacht, so bin ich um den Schlaf gebracht"* (Whenever I think of Germany at night, I am robbed of sleep).

Equally worrisome are the recent acts of xenophobia and the re-appearance of anti-Semitic acts and publications in Germany. However, on the other side of the ledger, I find encouragement in the spontaneity of mass demonstrations by hundreds of thousands of German citizens, young and old, who took to the streets and protested against renewed acts of terrorism in 1993. This never happened during the Weimar Republic. These demonstrations, as well as the fact that anti-Semitic and bigoted acts such as the denial of the Holocaust are prohibited in Germany, are an indication that democracy and the respect for human rights have taken root. The additional fact that today Germany has become one of the main pillars of the European Union seems to warrant the expectation that a relapse into the past is highly unlikely. Significantly, a Social Democratic member of the German parliament, in a recent speech at the Goethe Institute here in Los Angeles, suggested the following formula for German nationalism: *"Deutscher sein ist etwas Bestimmtes, aber nichts Besonderes"* (To be German is something specific, but nothing special).

I firmly believe that an ongoing dialogue between Germans and Jews, a joint endeavor to face the past with absolute candor and to build bridges of understanding for future generations, is an absolute necessity. I recently participated in the establishment of a group in Los Angeles named the German-American Cultural Society, which is dedicated to this very objective.

At a dinner party given by our gracious hostess, Margarete Hegardt, the Swedish Consul General in Hamburg, Germany, during my second wife Birgitta's and my visit to Hamburg in the summer of 1995, I had a most interesting discussion on this subject with the director of the Catholic Academy, in Hamburg, Dr. G. Gorschenek. This gentleman is committed to the challenging task of reconciliation between Christians and Jews in the wake of the two-thousand-year-old demonization of the Jews by the Church. I quote the following excerpt from the introduction of a book co-authored by him and Stephan Reimers and published on the occasion of the fiftieth anniversary of Kristallnacht in 1989. The book is entitled *Open Wounds, Burning Questions—Jews in Germany from 1938 until Today*:

> Even today, when Christians reflect upon guilt, suffering, and reconciliation in light of what happened, they must ask themselves how much and what kind of responsibility they bear. How could there be a solid foundation to the encounter between Christians and Jews as long as this question, which is still felt to be uncomfortable and painful inside and outside the Church, has not been answered?

My meeting with this gentleman and his honest attempt to strike at the roots of catastrophic events of our times have given me a great deal of encouragement.

C·h·a·p·t·e·r E·i·g·h·t
FAMILY, PHILOSOPHY, AND POLITICS

WHILE MY PROFESSIONAL LIFE has been fulfilling in terms of the challenges of which I believe I acquitted myself successfully, as well as from the perspective of many interesting human experiences which I have had, it was second in priority to the beautiful family life which it was my good fortune to enjoy, thanks to my beloved Ursula. She was the personification of the Hebrew concept of *Eshet Chayil*, a woman of valor. Throughout our fifty-year marriage, we truly shared all the joys and problems which came our way, first in Bolivia and then here in America. We grew up in the same environment and shared the same fate, which forged us together. Ursula's sound judgment and practical advice, both in matters of everyday life and in making decisions which were crucial to our future, were indispensable.

I vividly remember our discussion in Bolivia when I was offered a position with the American embassy. At the same time, I had received an offer from the Bolivian affiliate of the American Rubber Reserve Company to be the manager's assistant, at a much higher salary than that offered by the American embassy. Ursula and I felt strongly that, from a long-term perspective, employment with the U.S. embassy offered the opportunity for us to attain our goal of living in the United States.

We had two beautiful children, our first daughter, Gaby, and our "afterthought," Leslie Miriam, a "native" American who arrived upon the scene almost seventeen years later. We were proud of both daughters, who grew up to be wonderful human beings, and proud of our sons-in-law, Elie and Victor, who are excellent husbands and fathers. We were blessed with four lovely grandchildren, Danny, Michali, Tammy, and Julia. Shortly before I finished this autobiography, Michali presented me with my first great-granddaughter, Ariella Yael.

During most of our married life we shared our home with Ursula's parents. Thus three generations lived under one roof for many years. Ursula's parents helped us raise our children and were devoted grandparents. We certainly were a bilingual family and constantly switched from English into German and vice versa.

My beloved Ursula's passing in November 1989 after a long struggle with cancer, exactly one month after our fiftieth wedding anniversary, left me devastated, although during the last stages of her illness I tried to prepare myself for this event. During her two-year struggle we were on a constant emotional rollercoaster. We often talked about our youth in Breslau, the miracle of our escape from Germany, our children and grandchildren, and also about all of our relatives who had perished in the Holocaust. During one of these conversations—I believe it was in early 1989—Ursula remarked, "Even though I know that I won't live beyond sixty-eight years, I must be grateful for being a survivor, being able to save my parents, and for the blessings of a happy marriage and wonderful children and grandchildren." During the last few months before Ursula's passing, I often sought solace and strength in walks on the seashore. As I watched the sailboats slowly disappear on the horizon, I thought of Ursula, whose life was slowly ebbing away. I began to realize that the horizon of our vision does not necessarily mark the end of all existence. Still when the end came, everything around me seemed to collapse. Despite the wonderful support of my children, nothing could relieve the pain of an empty house that used to be a home.

As time went by I slowly began to realize that life is a gift to be shared with a loving person. I believe that if one is fortunate enough to find a person one learns to love and who appears to be a desirable partner for life's continuing journey, one should readily accept this precious gift.

I found this partner in Birgitta, whom I asked to marry me after three years of a beautiful friendship. During my hospitalization for heart surgery in May 1993, there was not a day when Birgitta, like the rest of my family, did not come to see me after finishing her classes at Cal State Northridge. It was during one of her visits that she literally saved my life when I collapsed in the hospital room. We got married on January 2, 1994. A new life started for me when we moved into our new home on Stradella Road in Bel Air.

Starting a new chapter in my life after so many happy years with Ursula was not easy. However, Birgitta's warmth, love, and understanding soon made me feel that I had truly found a new partner in life. The inside of our new house reflects Birgitta's sense of beauty and symmetry. She encouraged me to continue and conclude these memoirs.

She is mainly responsible for the extreme difficulty I experience in believing that my chronological age is seventy-eight.

Nevertheless, at this age one feels the need for introspection and some self-analysis.

What are the forces that shaped my thinking and my perspective?

Obviously, German culture, specifically German classics, such as Schiller and Goethe. German philosophers, particularly Immanuel Kant and his *Critiques of Pure and Practical Reason* had a significant impact on my intellectual orientation. I was also impressed by Schiller's advocacy of individual and collective freedom, and by Goethe's dramatization of man's perpetual struggle for redemption from the forces of evil in his *Faust*.

At the same time, I was fascinated by the French philosophers of the seventeenth and eighteenth centuries, particularly Descartes and Rousseau. I still vividly recall the time I read Rousseau's *Contrat Social*, its philosophy of the sovereignty of the people and the people's right to liberate themselves, by force if necessary, from tyrants.

The curriculum of the Johannes Gymnasium included the study of ancient Greek and Latin (nine years of Latin and six years of Greek). I enjoyed not only the study of these two languages but the world they unlocked, the world of Aeschylus, Euripides, Aristophanes, and the world of Socrates, Plato, and Aristotle. I was deeply impressed by the belief of these philosophers in man's ability to discover through scientific inquiry not only the laws of the physical world but the forces and processes that shape man's mind and soul, as well as the powers which do control and those which should control public institutions. Socrates words *"Gnoti s'auton"* (know thyself) postulate the need for introspection and understanding of the forces that live within us as the prerequisite for self-improvement. His defiance of mob rule and his refusal to recant, for which he paid with his life, represent the highest degree of *"Zivilcourage."*

I found it hard to understand how it came about that Germany, with its high appreciation of humanistic education, with its emphasis on the rule of law (*Rechtsstaat*) and human dignity, could create and raise a generation whose accomplishments included spreading terror across Europe and building and operating the death camps of Auschwitz and Treblinka. The apparent transmutation of many of my professors and schoolmates from civilized human beings into fanatical Hitler followers unfolded before my very eyes. Almost immediately after Hitler's assumption of power, many of my professors and fellow students, including many whom I had previously considered friends, appeared in Nazi uniforms with hobnailed boots and gave the Nazi salute at the beginning of class. One of our professors, who only a short time before had discussed Plato's *Apologia*, now cited certain passages of Homer's *Iliad* to prove that Homer had been one of the early advocates of the *Fuehrer* principle.

It was a tragic self-deception of my generation and those

preceding it to believe that the high moral standards set by the poets and thinkers of Germany governed the conduct of most of its citizens and that the Nazi movement was merely a temporary aberration.

But although the rather one-sided attempt at symbiosis between Jews and Germans ended in the worst tragedy in the annals of Jewish history since the destruction of the Second Temple, it brought forth a large number of distinguished men and women whose legacy and contribution to Jewish thought and to Western civilization will survive the ages.

One of these was Heinrich Graetz, the outstanding Jewish historian and author of the standard work *History of the Jews*, who taught at Breslau Theological Seminary toward the end of the nineteenth century. Another distinguished scholar whose knowledge and wisdom had a deep impact on me was Professor Isaac Heinemann, originally from Frankfurt, who taught at both the Jewish Theological Seminary and Breslau University. He was as much at home with Plato and Aristotle as he was with the world of the Talmud, Maimonides, and other Jewish philosophers. His publications and lectures on Hellenism and the Jewish philosopher Philo of Alexandria attracted Jewish and non-Jewish students, scholars as well as the general public.

I likewise remember Ephraim Urbach, who was one of my teachers at the seminary. He joined the faculty as a young man upon completion of his studies in Rome. I very much enjoyed his lectures on the Bible and specifically on the ethical teachings of the prophets. He went to Israel in the late 1930s and there joined the faculty of Hebrew University. I understand that he was even tapped to become president of Israel.

Our chief Rabbi, Dr. Hermann Vogelstein, who conducted our religious instruction at the Gymnasium, was the author of the scholarly work *History of the Jews in Rome*, which became one of the leading sources of reference on the subject.

Philosophers like Hermann Cohen, the Neo-Platonist, Martin Buber, Gershom Sholem, and the sainted Rabbi Leo Baeck, made lasting contributions to the German and Jewish culture.

Among those German-Jews of my generation and from my hometown whose talents benefitted America, their new home, is Walter Lacqueur, the noted historian, who was a schoolmate of mine at the Johannes Gymnasium.

When those among the German and Austrian Jews who succeeded in obtaining visas for overseas destinations left Germany, the baggage of a large number of them, including my own, contained the standard works of the German *Klassiker*. They brought their culture and customs with them as well. Many of them, like my own family, continued speaking German at home; and when they arrived at their destination, they sometimes compared conditions in their new countries to those prevailing in the *"Guten, alten Zeiten"* (Good old times in Germany): *"Bei uns in Deutschland"* or *"in Wien."*

Thus the German and Austrian Jews who had been driven out of the countries of their birth became what Germans call *Kulturtraeger*, transmitters of German culture at its best in their new countries, in very much the same way in which the Spanish Jews after their expulsion from Spain in 1492 perpetuated the Spanish language of that era (Ladino) in the countries to which they emigrated. The liturgy practiced in the Sephardic temples around the world vividly reflects this tradition.

Our oldest daughter, Gaby, who has never been to Germany and who was born in Bolivia, speaks German fluently; our youngest daughter Leslie, who was born in Los Angeles, understands it.

At an early age, while attending the Gymnasium, I developed a very keen interest in foreign languages, specifically French, but also Italian and Spanish. Having studied Latin for many years, I was fascinated by the development of these languages from one common root. After living over three quarters of a century, I find that during my own lifetime the languages which I studied during my youth have undergone profound changes. Many new words and expressions have sprung up, and many words have changed their meanings. Obviously, a language is a living organism, reflecting constantly changing images and thought-patterns.

To my study of the Romance languages I added Polish and

later, in South America, Russian. I also added the study of Japanese after my first trip to Japan in 1956. Unfortunately, little has remained of my knowledge and proficiency in Japanese and Russian, due to lack of practice. My study of Hebrew, which I commenced when I was about nine years of age, I later expanded when I studied modern Hebrew and Hebrew literature. My favorite writers, whose thoughts influenced a new generation of pioneers in Israel, are Achad Haam, Chaim Nachman Bialik, and Agnon.

From the beginning of my linguistic studies I always felt that a language is much more than just a means of communication. I always considered the study of a language as the acquisition of a key which opens the gate of understanding to a different culture. If events in Germany had not turned out the way they did, I probably would have become a philologist, teaching languages or history and philosophy.

Later on, while living in Arequipa, Peru, and subsequently during my first few years in La Paz working for two prominent import-export firms, my knowledge of languages not only greatly facilitated my introduction to international trade, but also opened access to a substantial number of interesting people from different parts of the world. My ability to take shorthand in all of the languages which I had learned while still in Germany also proved to be quite an advantage. My subsequent experiences in international banking and, later on, as export-import manager of a steel company with worldwide marketing responsibilities, convinced me that the gradual breakdown of trade barriers and restrictions on international commerce and the ability of people all over the world to communicate and to trade freely with each other serves the enlightened self-interest of each nation. It gives their populations access to goods and services at the most competitive prices, and thus raises their standard of living. The best example in support of this philosophy is the emergence and development of the European Union, which arose from the modest beginnings of the European Coal and Steel Community, a treaty between Germany and France, the old arch-enemies. I believe that the opening of markets in the Middle

East, enabling Israel and its Arab neighbors to trade freely with one another and to exchange technological know-how, will be one of the most important milestones on the way to peace in the area. As one of the founders of several international chambers of commerce here in California, as director and president of the Foreign Trade Association of Southern California, chairman and director of the International Section of the Los Angeles County Bar Association, and as cofounder of the Center for International Commercial Arbitration here in Los Angeles, I have tried to make modest contributions towards the realization of this goal.

My life in South America left me with an abiding interest in the political-economic development of that continent. In the early 1960s I taught several extension courses at UCLA on "Latin American Relations." My students and I had formed such a close relationship that when I had to discontinue the course as a result of the development of my law practice, they asked me to meet with them for dinner and subsequent informal discussion at somebody's home once a month. This discussion group became an inspiration to all of us. I suspect that, like a large number of teachers, I learned at least as much from my students, their questions, and their insights, as they learned from me.

Politically, my family and I have been sympathizers with the philosophy of the Democratic Party, which we joined immediately after becoming citizens in 1950. We were impressed with the Democratic Party's progressive record in the field of socioeconomic policy: social security, the eight-hour workday, minimum wages, workman's compensation and, subsequently, medicare and human rights laws. All of this legislation has passed by Democrat-controlled Congresses under the leadership of Democratic presidents and against the bitter opposition of special interests. Ursula and I became quite active as organizers of and active participants in the California Democratic Committees (CDC), a democratic grassroots movement which sprang up in California in the late 1950s.

Our affiliation with the philosophy of the Democratic

Party was considerably strengthened by the personal impact of Democratic leaders, specifically Eleanor Roosevelt, Hubert Humphrey, and Adlai Stevenson. We met Eleanor Roosevelt after a Democratic rally in Pasadena in the early 1960s, where she discussed her impressions gathered during a trip to Eastern Europe and the Soviet Union. Her address reflected her deep concern about human rights in the Soviet-controlled countries of Eastern Europe.

Hubert Humphrey impressed us as a champion of human rights at the 1948 Democratic Convention. Several years later I had a conversation with him during a reception at the Beverly Wilshire Hotel in Beverly Hills, California, before his appearance as keynote speaker at a rally of the Friends of Histadruth (Israeli Labor Party). When I asked him about the reason for his support of Israel, he replied, "I believe in Israel as a sincere friend of the United States, the only democratic country in that part of the world. You can rest assured that my friendship for Israel is not gaining me any votes in the State of Minnesota."

Adlai Stevenson, former governor of the State of Illinois, twice defeated in the presidential elections of 1952 and 1956, impressed us with his appeal for a reasoned debate in the political arena and for continuation of Democratic policies at a time when America was going through the darkest days of McCarthyism.

In light of my own experience in Latin America, where I witnessed the abysmal misery of the masses on a day-to-day basis, I was deeply impressed by the "Alliance for Progress" program for Latin America which John F. Kennedy announced shortly after becoming president in 1961. This project, unlike its forerunners, sought to create a true partnership between the people of the United States and the Latin American nations for the purpose of raising their socio-economic infrastructure. Although the United States government was to fund the bulk of the program, its implementation was to be carried out by the private sector of each country in cooperation with their respective governments. Its basic concept, like that of JFK's

Peace Corps, was the involvement of private citizens in the worldwide efforts of the United States to improve living standards in the emerging countries.

In the second half of 1962, a friend of mine with close ties to the Rand Corporation in Santa Monica told me that he had joined a group of volunteers in an effort to come up with ideas for the implementation of the Alliance for Progress program. He added that this group was in communication with the White House through Arthur Schlesinger, the historian and mentor of JFK, who was in charge of reporting to the president on the progress of the program. My friend suggested that, in view of my experience gained while living in South America and working for the United States, I should be able to make a contribution to the project. I readily joined this group and was introduced to a number of interesting young men who were experts in the fields of world economics and technology. We usually met at least three times a month in the evenings, and our meetings lasted until the early morning hours. Some of these men had previously prepared and carried out economic and technical projects in several countries. I remember one of them who had been in charge of an electrification plan for a part of Greece on behalf of the Rand Corporation. Others had assisted certain countries in the Middle East in updating their traffic-control systems.

After a few months we had completed our plan of action, consisting of assignments given to each of us and of the coordination of our work. I was in charge of outlining plans for the improvement of the educational systems in Bolivia, Peru, and Equador.

Several months later all of us handed in our outlines to the member of our group who was in direct contact with Arthur Schlesinger. I still remember the electrifying news a few weeks later that the president, to whom Arthur Schlesinger had submitted our outlines, was giving us the green light on the completion of the detailed plan.

Unfortunately, the tragic event in Dallas on November 22, 1963, ended this project and the "Alliance for Progress."

FREEDOM AND RELIGION

I AM DEEPLY GRATEFUL to this country, which became my home many years ago, for the opportunities I found here. I do not believe it would have been possible for me to study law anywhere else while at the same time holding a full-time position in business. This is only one example of the freedoms which the individual enjoys in this society, allowing him to pursue whatever goal he chooses. To the extent that there are any obstacles on account of a person's race, religion, or ethnic origin, the process of exposing and removing these barriers is in progress and will not be stopped.

These freedoms are appreciated much more by those who came here than by those who were born here. This is best highlighted by the fact that America has one of the lowest voter turnout records among democratic nations. As immigrants born in a country where we were disenfranchised, we eagerly looked forward to the day when we would be able to exercise the highest privilege of a citizen in a democratic country: The right to vote. Neither my family nor I have missed an election since we acquired citizenship almost fifty years ago.

One feature that impresses me in the American character is pragmatism. Like other former Europeans, I am prone to discuss political, economic, and other problems from the standpoint of ideology and to theorize on their solutions. In contrast with this habit, I have found the American search for practical solutions, unencumbered by ideological or theoretical ballast, a most valuable guide. The motto "the proof of the pudding is in the eating" sums it all up.

And yet many strains of clashing colors are woven into the fabric of the American character, which should be redefined in light of the demographic pastiche which characterizes American society of the mid 1990s. The term "rugged individualism" is often used to describe a society in which everyone has a right to "do his own thing." Yet one finds few places in the Western world where there is a greater degree of conformity of conduct in almost all spheres of life.

In a democratic country such as ours, we are expected to express "politically correct" views; behavior is shaped by "peer pressure." In business, one cannot expect to rise through the ranks unless one conforms to a set pattern of views, conduct, and attire established by the corporate hierarchy, as described by William White in his *The Organization Man* many years ago.

An independent judiciary is one of the cornerstones of the American Constitution and of the constitutions of the different states of the union. And yet state judges are elected like candidates for political office, subject to re-election after their terms expire. It is obvious that their chances of re-election depend on the popularity rather than on the legal soundness of their decisions.

Americans are among the most generous people, both collectively and individually. When disaster strikes here or abroad, Americans will respond with immediate relief. To give a personal example, one hour after the big earthquake that struck Los Angeles at 4:00 A.M. on January 17, 1994, which was about ten hours after we had moved into our new residence, there was a knock on our door. When I answered, there was a man outside introducing himself as our neighbor and asking us whether we were all right and offering us a flashlight. To us this was a touching example of the spontaneous generosity with which the average American treats his neighbor in the face of a calamity.

And yet America and South Africa are the only civilized countries which, for lack of a national health-coverage system, have let millions of their own citizens live or vegetate without adequate medical care or any care at all.

The dichotomy in the political arena is just as rampant. For many years the cry "let's get the government off our backs" has been heard with ever-increasing intensity. Yet many, if not most, of the same people who vigorously oppose governmental "interference" want to move governmental intrusion from the boardroom into the bedroom by prohibiting abortion. To go one step further, many of the so-called "pro-lifers" care more about human beings before birth than after. This was manifested by their opposition to benefits to unwed mothers and their children.

As I look at American society in the 1990s, I see it fragmenting into a large number of ethnic groups with nothing in common, not even language. When my wife Ursula and I came to this country over fifty years ago, we were accompanied by her parents, who did not speak English. One of the first steps they took was to enroll in evening courses of "English for the Foreign Born." They attended these courses five nights a week after work, motivated by the desire to communicate with the people around them, their future fellow-citizens, and to integrate themselves into American society as quickly as possible. They shared these aspirations with most of those who arrived on these shores. They all considered the efforts required to learn English a small price to pay for the privilege of becoming citizens of this country. I vividly remember one evening several months after our arrival in California when my in-laws proudly announced at the dinner table that they were now able to understand most of the contents of the *Los Angeles Times*.

As to the religious forces which shaped my philosophy, it was the message of Judaism—the proclamation of the oneness of the Supreme Being, combined with the demand for ethical conduct of one's life and the practice of social justice—that had a lasting impact on my thinking. Outside of the Bible I have found no better expression of this concept than Goethe's words at the conclusion of the second part of *Faust*: *"Wer immer strebend sich bemueht, den koennen wir erloesen."* ("Those who constantly strive for perfection we can redeem.") Indeed, my studies of the Bible and its commentaries, as well as of the legal systems of the Western world, which are founded on the Bible, convinced me that the word *justice* is written in Hebrew letters.

For many years I have tried to understand what has been the secret of our survival as Jews for 2,000 years of stateless-ness—most of the time as pariahs. This is a question that has concerned and confounded friend and foe alike, lately even the Dalai Lama of Tibet in quest of our "secret formula," which he hopes might help his own people overcome their present adversities.

Those of us who know the story of Rabbi Yochanan ben Sakkai, who, after escaping besieged Jerusalem in a coffin, appeared before the Roman general and requested permission to build an academy at Yavneh, have the answer.

After the fall of Jerusalem and Judaea, the Torah and the oral laws implementing it became the "portable fatherland" of the Jews, their spiritual compass in the diaspora until the messianic age when God would take them back to the land of Israel. Sustained by the hope of ultimate redemption and united by a spiritual heritage, the Jews accomplished a miracle unique in world history: they survived the destruction of their land and their expulsion from it for almost two thousand years of persecution, and the Holocaust that resulted in the annihilation of one third of our people.

While the Bible postulates that God created man and woman in His image it became clear to me during my study of the scriptures that we human beings created God in our image, and that as we passed through different stages of development, so did our deity.

The God of Israel was originally a tribal God, believed to be confined to territorial boundaries; thus Jonah believed that he could escape Him by taking off on a ship bound for a foreign destination. This god later became the universal God of the prophets, whose vision was that of justice and universal peace among nations. People's visions of their deity or deities tells us much more about the people themselves than about their deity.

During my studies of philosophy I was fascinated by the "Ethics" of Baruch Spinoza, the Jewish lens-grinder who lived in Amsterdam during the seventeenth century, whose "heretical" ideas about God resulted in his excommunication from the Jewish community.

The God of Spinoza is not the father figure who rules over us and possesses human qualities such as goodness, compassion, and justice. Rather, the God of Spinoza exists eternally and immutably. Human beings are but a transient form of the divine spark. God represents the universal process, the energy permeating the universe, the *elan vital* of Henri Bergson. He is the fountainhead of all laws ruling the physical, the intellectual, and the spiritual world, forever incomprehensible to the limited minds of human beings. I am reminded of the words "I am who I am," with which God identified Himself to Moses.

And yet despite my attempts to disassociate myself from the idea of a personal God, there have been times in my own life when I have felt a protective hand over me.

I vividly remember November 10, 1938, the terrible day following Kristallnacht. On my way to the railroad station in an attempt to escape to Berlin, I ran into a howling Nazi mob. They followed a group of SS men who drove a large number of Jews toward the railroad cars to take them to the Buchenwald concentration camp. How it was possible for me, carrying my suitcase to walk right past them, I will never understand.

The next "miracle" that saved me occurred in Osnabrueck, Germany, where the Dutch border police, who had refused to let me enter Holland, shipped me back on December 22, 1938 into the waiting arms of the Gestapo, who were anxious to take me to a concentration camp. Never in my life, not even during my professional life as an attorney, did I manifest such powers of persuasion as I possessed when I convinced the Gestapo to release me so that I could take the night train from Osnabrueck to Hamburg.

In 1940 another incredible event occurred. Ursula and I had obtained new Bolivian visas for my mother and Ursula's parents and, in the middle of the war with the help of the "Hilfsverein" (Jewish Aid Society), we arranged for their transport across Eastern Europe to Moscow, thence via trans-Siberian railroad to Vladivostock. There they took the ferry to Korea and Japan. From Kobe, Japan, they sailed to Arica, Chile, halfway around the world, where they disembarked and took the train to La Paz, passing an altitude of over 16,000 feet. The question remains: Was all of that accomplished by human effort alone?

Later on, in 1948, when I witnessed the rebirth of the Jewish people in their own land, and subsequently, in 1967 after the triumph of Israel's army over its enemies in the face of overwhelming odds, we all felt that we were witnessing a miracle equal in significance to that of the Maccabees over 2,000 years ago.

If Judaism had remained a monolithic religion consisting mainly of a rigid set of rules, the Jewish people would have disappeared a long time ago. From the time of Hillel and Shammai it has been our mental flexibility, our ability to confront change, to absorb different schools of thought and practices, to maintain our heritage as well as a universal perspective, and to preserve hope for our redemption—it is all of these things that have given the Jewish people their unique vitality. This is a gift which we acknowledge in prayers by thanking the Supreme Being for having "planted eternal life in our midst."

Why am I chronicling the events of my life? When the idea of writing my memoirs first came to my mind, I thought that it might be of purely personal interest to my children and grandchildren. However, as time went on I realized that my life and the events which I experienced made me one of the representatives of a generation of German Jews who witnessed (and survived) the cataclysmic end of an historic experiment that began with the emancipation of Jews in Germany in 1812 and ended tragically in 1933. Since destiny bestowed on me (for no apparent reason) the gift of surviving this catastrophe, I feel that I have an obligation and a responsibility to bear witness to these events. I believe I owe this responsibility not only to my family, but also to future generations, particularly of Jews and Germans and possibly to historians in search of source material. The recent appearance of so-called "revisionist" history, which seeks to trivialize, distort, or even deny the events witnessed by me and other survivors, as well as the significance of these events, seems to reinforce this obligation.

My generation witnessed humankind's deepest fall into the abyss of man's inhumanity to man. However, we should never forget the outstanding examples of greatness and courage of those men and women in all countries of Nazi-occupied Europe, some in Germany itself, who at the risk of their own lives saved Jewish fellow citizens from the fate of the "final solution." Their example reminds me of Leo Tolstoy's words in *The Kreutzer Sonata:* "And a light shines in the darkness."

EPILOGUE

WHEN THE CHINESE WISH to lay a curse on someone, they say "May he live in interesting times." While I certainly have lived in interesting times, I feel blessed, not cursed.

Fifty years of my life I shared with my beloved Ursula. Together we started a new life, first in South America and afterwards in this beautiful country. As I am about to reach biblical age, I am blessed by a loving family of children and grandchildren and by the company of my dearest Birgitta, who has given me a new home. Her creativity and expertise in the world of art have been an inspiration to me. Without her encouragement to go on with this memoir when my will seemed to be flagging, this autobiography would not have been completed.

At almost eighty I am still in the mainstream of life, maintaining a full-time practice of my profession as a lawyer, and enjoying the company of interesting people, good books, music, learning, and teaching. This includes the Monday morning study group sessions at which, under the inspiring guidance of Rabbi Brander, we study Talmudic texts. Above all, I enjoy my daily walks with Birgitta and my weekly bike rides along the beach. Reflecting upon how best to summarize the lessons that my life's experiences have taught me and my generation, I am tempted to quote one of our sages, Hillel, who lived over 2,000 years ago:

If I am not for myself, who is?
And if I am for myself alone, what am I?